AF680652

# Tax Credits Act 2002

**CHAPTER 21**

---

Explanatory Notes are available separately

---

**GRANGIS UK Publishing**

Adapted and published by GRANGIS (Grand Register Library).
Online: www.grangis.com
E-mail: contact@grangis.com


In this version:
ISBN: 979-8-88559-046-4

Note: This is the original version (as it was originally enacted). Title, sub-title and the generated date is as marked on the pages.

# Tax Credits Act 2002

## CHAPTER 21

## TAX CREDITS ACT 2002

### PART 1

TAX CREDITS

*General*



*Child tax credit*



*Working tax credit*



*Rate*

*Decisions*



*Payment*



*Penalties*



*Fraud*



*Interest*



*Appeals*



*Supplementary*

## PART 2

### CHILD BENEFIT AND GUARDIAN'S ALLOWANCE

*Transfer of functions etc.*



*Minor amendments*



## PART 3

### SUPPLEMENTARY

*Information etc.*



*Other supplementary provisions*



---

## SCHEDULES

# Tax Credits Act 2002

**2002 CHAPTER 21**

An Act to make provision for tax credits; to amend the law about child benefit and guardian's allowance; and for connected purposes. [8th July 2002]

BE IT ENACTED by the Queen's most Excellent Majesty, by and with the advice and consent of the Lords Spiritual and Temporal, and Commons, in this present Parliament assembled, and by the authority of the same, as follows:—

## PART 1

TAX CREDITS

*General*

### 1 Introductory

(1) This Act makes provision for—

(a) a tax credit to be known as child tax credit, and

(b) a tax credit to be known as working tax credit.

(2) In this Act references to a tax credit are to either of those tax credits and references to tax credits are to both of them.

(3) The following (which are superseded by tax credits) are abolished—

(a) children's tax credit under section 257AA of the Income and Corporation Taxes Act 1988 (c. 1),

(b) working families' tax credit,

(c) disabled person's tax credit,

(d) the amounts which, in relation to income support and income-based jobseeker's allowance, are prescribed as part of the applicable amount in respect of a child or young person, the family premium, the enhanced disability premium in respect of a child or young person and the disabled child premium,

(e) increases in benefits in respect of children under sections 80 and 90 of the Social Security Contributions and Benefits Act 1992 (c. 4) and sections 80 and 90 of the Social Security Contributions and Benefits (Northern Ireland) Act 1992 (c. 7), and

(f) the employment credit under the schemes under section 2(2) of the Employment and Training Act 1973 (c. 50) and section 1 of the Employment and Training Act (Northern Ireland) 1950 (c. 29 (N.I.)) known as "New Deal 50plus".

## 2 Functions of Board

(1) Tax credits are to be under the care and management of the Board.

(2) Section 10 of the Exchequer and Audit Departments Act 1866 (c. 39) (gross revenues to be paid to Exchequer) is to be construed as allowing the Board to deduct payments for or in respect of tax credits before causing the gross revenues of their department to be paid to the account mentioned in that section.

(3) For the purposes of the Inland Revenue Regulation Act 1890 (c. 21) the definition of "inland revenue" in section 39 of that Act is to be taken to include tax credits.

(4) The reference in section 4(1) of that Act (appointment of collectors, officers and other persons) to collecting, receiving, managing and accounting for inland revenue is to be taken to include a reference to paying and managing tax credits.

(5) The duties of the Board under section 13 of that Act (Board to keep accounts) are to include a duty to set forth in the accounts mentioned in that section—

(a) the amounts of the several payments made by them of or in respect of tax credits,

(b) the amounts of the expenses of paying and managing tax credits, and

(c) the amounts received by them in respect of tax credits,

distinguishing in each case between amounts relating to child tax credit and amounts relating to working tax credit.

(6) In any declaration for the purposes of section 6 of the Taxes Management Act 1970 (c. 9) (declarations on taking office), whether made before or after the commencement of this section, the reference to an offence relating to inland revenue is to be taken to include a reference to an offence relating to a tax credit.

## 3 Claims

(1) Entitlement to a tax credit for the whole or part of a tax year is dependent on the making of a claim for it.

(2) Where the Board—

(a) decide under section 14 not to make an award of a tax credit on a claim, or

(b) decide under section 16 to terminate an award of a tax credit made on a claim,

(subject to any appeal) any entitlement, or subsequent entitlement, to the tax credit for any part of the same tax year is dependent on the making of a new claim.

(3) A claim for a tax credit may be made—

(a) jointly by the members of a married couple or unmarried couple both of whom are aged at least sixteen and are in the United Kingdom, or
(b) by a person who is aged at least sixteen and is in the United Kingdom but is not entitled to make a claim under paragraph (a) (jointly with another).

(4) Entitlement to a tax credit pursuant to a claim ceases—
(a) in the case of a joint claim, if the persons by whom it was made could no longer jointly make a joint claim, and
(b) in the case of a single claim, if the person by whom it was made could no longer make a single claim.

(5) In this Part "married couple" means a man and woman who are married to each other and are neither—
(a) separated under a court order, nor
(b) separated in circumstances in which the separation is likely to be permanent.

(6) In this Part "unmarried couple" means a man and a woman who are not a married couple but are living together as husband and wife.

(7) Circumstances may be prescribed in which a person is to be treated for the purposes of this Part as being, or as not being, in the United Kingdom.

(8) In this Part—
"joint claim" means a claim under paragraph (a) of subsection (3), and
"single claim" means a claim under paragraph (b) of that subsection.

## 4 Claims: supplementary

(1) Regulations may—
(a) require a claim for a tax credit to be made in a prescribed manner and within a prescribed time,
(b) provide for a claim for a tax credit made in prescribed circumstances to be treated as having been made on a prescribed date earlier or later than that on which it is made,
(c) provide that, in prescribed circumstances, a claim for a tax credit may be made for a period wholly or partly after the date on which it is made,
(d) provide that, in prescribed circumstances, an award on a claim for a tax credit may be made subject to the condition that the requirements for entitlement are satisfied at a prescribed time,
(e) provide for a claim for a tax credit to be made or proceeded with in the name of a person who has died,
(f) provide that, in prescribed circumstances, one person may act for another in making a claim for a tax credit,
(g) provide that, in prescribed circumstances, a claim for a tax credit made by one member of a married couple or an unmarried couple is to be treated as also made by the other member of the married couple or unmarried couple, and
(h) provide that a claim for a tax credit is to be treated as made by a person or persons in such other circumstances as may be prescribed.

(2) The Board may supply to a person who has made a claim for a tax credit (whether or not jointly with another)—

(a) any information relating to the claim, to an award made on the claim or to any change of circumstances relevant to the claim or such an award,

(b) any communication made or received relating to such an award or any such change of circumstances, and

(c) any other information which is relevant to any entitlement to tax credits pursuant to the claim or any such change of circumstances or which appeared to be so relevant at the time the information was supplied.

## 5 Period of awards

(1) Where a tax credit is claimed for a tax year by making a claim before the tax year begins, any award of the tax credit on the claim is for the whole of the tax year.

(2) An award on any other claim for a tax credit is for the period beginning with the date on which the claim is made and ending at the end of the tax year in which that date falls.

(3) Subsections (1) and (2) are subject to any decision by the Board under section 16 to terminate an award.

## 6 Notifications of changes of circumstances

(1) Regulations may provide that any change of circumstances of a prescribed description which may increase the maximum rate at which a person or persons may be entitled to a tax credit is to do so only if notification of it has been given.

(2) Regulations under subsection (1) may—

(a) provide for notification of a change of circumstances given in prescribed circumstances to be treated as having been given on a prescribed date earlier or later than that on which it is given,

(b) provide that, in prescribed circumstances, a notification of a change of circumstances may be given for a period wholly or partly after the date on which it is given, and

(c) provide that, in prescribed circumstances, an amendment of an award of a tax credit in consequence of a notification of a change of circumstances may be made subject to the condition that the requirements for entitlement to the amended amount of the tax credit are satisfied at a prescribed time.

(3) Regulations may require that, where a person has or persons have claimed a tax credit, notification is to be given if there is a change of circumstances of a prescribed description which may decrease the rate at which he is or they are entitled to the tax credit or mean that he ceases or they cease to be entitled to the tax credit.

(4) Regulations under this section may—

(a) require a notification to be given in a prescribed manner and within a prescribed time,

(b) specify the person or persons by whom a notification may be, or is to be, given, and

(c) provide that, in prescribed circumstances, one person may act for another in giving a notification.

## 7 Income test

(1) The entitlement of a person or persons of any description to a tax credit is dependent on the relevant income—

(a) not exceeding the amount determined in the manner prescribed for the purposes of this paragraph in relation to the tax credit and a person or persons of that description (referred to in this Part as the income threshold), or

(b) exceeding the income threshold by only so much that a determination in accordance with regulations under section 13(2) provides a rate of the tax credit in his or their case.

(2) Subsection (1) does not apply in relation to the entitlement of a person or persons to a tax credit for so long as the person, or either of the persons, is entitled to any social security benefit prescribed for the purposes of this subsection in relation to the tax credit.

(3) In this Part "the relevant income" means—

(a) if an amount is prescribed for the purposes of this paragraph and the current year income exceeds the previous year income by not more than that amount, the previous year income,

(b) if an amount is prescribed for the purposes of this paragraph and the current year income exceeds the previous year income by more than that amount, the current year income reduced by that amount,

(c) if an amount is prescribed for the purposes of this paragraph and the previous year income exceeds the current year income by not more than that amount, the previous year income,

(d) if an amount is prescribed for the purposes of this paragraph and the previous year income exceeds the current year income by more than that amount, the current year income increased by that amount, and

(e) otherwise, the current year income.

(4) In this Part "the current year income" means—

(a) in relation to persons by whom a joint claim for a tax credit is made, the aggregate income of the persons for the tax year to which the claim relates, and

(b) in relation to a person by whom a single claim for a tax credit is made, the income of the person for that tax year.

(5) In this Part "the previous year income" means—

(a) in relation to persons by whom a joint claim for a tax credit is made, the aggregate income of the persons for the tax year preceding that to which the claim relates, and

(b) in relation to a person by whom a single claim for a tax credit is made, the income of the person for that preceding tax year.

(6) Regulations may provide that, for the purposes of this Part, income of a prescribed description is to be treated as being, or as not being, income for a particular tax year.

(7) In particular, regulations may provide that income of a prescribed description of a person for the tax year immediately before the preceding tax year referred to in subsection (5) is to be treated as being income of that preceding tax year (instead of any actual income of that description of the person for that preceding tax year).

(8) Regulations may for the purposes of this Part make provision—

(a) as to what is, or is not, income, and
(b) as to the calculation of income.

(9) Regulations may provide that, for the purposes of this Part, a person is to be treated—
(a) as having income which he does not in fact have, or
(b) as not having income which he does in fact have.

(10) The Board may estimate the amount of the income of a person, or the aggregate income of persons, for any tax year for the purpose of making, amending or terminating an award of a tax credit; but such an estimate does not affect the rate at which he is, or they are, entitled to the tax credit for that or any other tax year.

*Child tax credit*

## 8 Entitlement

(1) The entitlement of the person or persons by whom a claim for child tax credit has been made is dependent on him, or either or both of them, being responsible for one or more children or qualifying young persons.

(2) Regulations may make provision for the purposes of child tax credit as to the circumstances in which a person is or is not responsible for a child or qualifying young person.

(3) For the purposes of this Part a person is a child if he has not attained the age of sixteen; but regulations may make provision for a person who has attained that age to remain a child for the purposes of this Part after attaining that age for a prescribed period or until a prescribed date.

(4) In this Part "qualifying young person" means a person, other than a child, who—
(a) has not attained such age (greater than sixteen) as is prescribed, and
(b) satisfies prescribed conditions.

(5) Circumstances may be prescribed in which a person is to be entitled to child tax credit for a prescribed period in respect of a child or qualifying young person who has died.

## 9 Maximum rate

(1) The maximum rate at which a person or persons may be entitled to child tax credit is to be determined in the prescribed manner.

(2) The prescribed manner of determination must involve the inclusion of—
(a) an element which is to be included in the case of all persons entitled to child tax credit, and
(b) an element in respect of each child or qualifying young person for whom the person is, or either or both of them is or are, responsible.

(3) The element specified in paragraph (a) of subsection (2) is to be known as the family element of child tax credit and that specified in paragraph (b) of that subsection is to be known as the individual element of child tax credit.

(4) The prescribed manner of determination may involve the inclusion of such other elements as may be prescribed.

(5) The prescribed manner of determination—

(a) may include provision for the amount of the family element of child tax credit to vary according to the age of any of the children or qualifying young persons or according to any such other factors as may be prescribed,

(b) may include provision for the amount of the individual element of child tax credit to vary according to the age of the child or qualifying young person or according to any such other factors as may be prescribed, and

(c) must include provision for the amount of the individual element of child tax credit to be increased in the case of a child or qualifying young person who is disabled and to be further increased in the case of a child or qualifying young person who is severely disabled.

(6) A child or qualifying young person is disabled, or severely disabled, for the purposes of this section only if—

(a) he satisfies prescribed conditions, or

(b) prescribed conditions exist in relation to him.

(7) If, in accordance with regulations under section 8(2), more than one claimant may be entitled to child tax credit in respect of the same child or qualifying young person, the prescribed manner of determination may include provision for the amount of any element of child tax credit included in the case of any one or more of them to be less than it would be if only one claimant were so entitled.

(8) "Claimant" means—

(a) in the case of a single claim, the person who makes the claim, and

(b) in the case of a joint claim, the persons who make the claim.

*Working tax credit*

## 10 Entitlement

(1) The entitlement of the person or persons by whom a claim for working tax credit has been made is dependent on him, or either or both of them, being engaged in qualifying remunerative work.

(2) Regulations may for the purposes of this Part make provision—

(a) as to what is, or is not, qualifying remunerative work, and

(b) as to the circumstances in which a person is, or is not, engaged in it.

(3) The circumstances prescribed under subsection (2)(b) may differ by reference to—

(a) the age of the person or either of the persons,

(b) whether the person, or either of the persons, is disabled,

(c) whether the person, or either of the persons, is responsible for one or more children or qualifying young persons, or

(d) any other factors.

(4) Regulations may make provision for the purposes of working tax credit as to the circumstances in which a person is or is not responsible for a child or qualifying young person.

## 11 Maximum rate

(1) The maximum rate at which a person or persons may be entitled to working tax credit is to be determined in the prescribed manner.

(2) The prescribed manner of determination must involve the inclusion of an element which is to be included in the case of all persons entitled to working tax credit.

(3) The prescribed manner of determination must also involve the inclusion of an element in respect of the person, or either or both of the persons, engaged in qualifying remunerative work—

(a) having a physical or mental disability which puts him at a disadvantage in getting a job, and

(b) satisfying such other conditions as may be prescribed.

(4) The element specified in subsection (2) is to be known as the basic element of working tax credit and the element specified in subsection (3) is to be known as the disability element of working tax credit.

(5) The prescribed manner of determination may involve the inclusion of such other elements as may be prescribed.

(6) The other elements may (in particular) include—

(a) an element in respect of the person, or either of the persons or the two of them taken together, being engaged in qualifying remunerative work to an extent prescribed for the purposes of this paragraph,

(b) an element in respect of the persons being the members of a married couple or an unmarried couple,

(c) an element in respect of the person not being a member of a married couple or an unmarried couple but being responsible for a child or qualifying young person,

(d) an element in respect of the person, or either or both of the persons, being severely disabled, and

(e) an element in respect of the person, or either or both of the persons, being over a prescribed age, satisfying prescribed conditions and having been engaged in qualifying remunerative work for not longer than a prescribed period.

(7) A person has a physical or mental disability which puts him at a disadvantage in getting a job, or is severely disabled, for the purposes of this section only if—

(a) he satisfies prescribed conditions, or

(b) prescribed conditions exist in relation to him.

## 12 Child care element

(1) The prescribed manner of determination of the maximum rate at which a person or persons may be entitled to working tax credit may involve the inclusion, in prescribed circumstances, of a child care element.

(2) A child care element is an element in respect of a prescribed proportion of so much of any relevant child care charges as does not exceed a prescribed amount.

(3) "Child care charges" are charges of a prescribed description incurred in respect of child care by the person, or either or both of the persons, by whom a claim for working tax credit is made.

(4) "Child care", in relation to a person or persons, means care provided—

(a) for a child of a prescribed description for whom the person is responsible, or for whom either or both of the persons is or are responsible, and

(b) by a person of a prescribed description.

(5) The descriptions of persons prescribed under subsection (4)(b) may include descriptions of persons approved in accordance with a scheme made by the appropriate national authority under this subsection.

(6) "The appropriate national authority" means—

(a) in relation to care provided in England, the Secretary of State,

(b) in relation to care provided in Scotland, the Scottish Ministers,

(c) in relation to care provided in Wales, the National Assembly for Wales, and

(d) in relation to care provided in Northern Ireland, the Department of Health, Social Services and Public Safety.

(7) The provision made by a scheme under subsection (5) must involve the giving of approvals, in accordance with criteria determined by or under the scheme, by such of the following as the scheme specifies—

(a) the appropriate national authority making the scheme,

(b) one or more specified persons or bodies or persons or bodies of a specified description, and

(c) persons or bodies accredited under the scheme in accordance with criteria determined by or under it.

(8) A scheme under subsection (5) may authorise—

(a) the making of grants or loans to, and

(b) the charging of reasonable fees by,

persons and bodies giving approvals.

*Rate*

## 13 Rate

(1) Where, in the case of a person or persons entitled to a tax credit, the relevant income does not exceed the income threshold (or his or their entitlement arises by virtue of section 7(2)), the rate at which he is or they are entitled to the tax credit is the maximum rate for his or their case.

(2) Regulations shall make provision as to the manner of determining the rate (if any) at which a person is, or persons are, entitled to a tax credit in any other case.

(3) The manner of determination prescribed under subsection (2)—

(a) may involve the making of adjustments so as to avoid fractional amounts, and

(b) may include provision for securing that, where the rate at which a person or persons would be entitled to a tax credit would be less than a prescribed rate, there is no rate in his or their case.

*Decisions*

### 14 Initial decisions

(1) On a claim for a tax credit the Board must decide—

(a) whether to make an award of the tax credit, and

(b) if so, the rate at which to award it.

(2) Before making their decision the Board may by notice—

(a) require the person, or either or both of the persons, by whom the claim is made to provide any information or evidence which the Board consider they may need for making their decision, or

(b) require any person of a prescribed description to provide any information or evidence of a prescribed description which the Board consider they may need for that purpose,

by the date specified in the notice.

(3) The Board's power to decide the rate at which to award a tax credit includes power to decide to award it at a nil rate.

### 15 Revised decisions after notifications

(1) Where notification of a change of circumstances increasing the maximum rate at which a person or persons may be entitled to a tax credit is given in accordance with regulations under section 6(1), the Board must decide whether (and, if so, how) to amend the award of the tax credit made to him or them.

(2) Before making their decision the Board may by notice—

(a) require the person by whom the notification is given to provide any information or evidence which the Board consider they may need for making their decision, or

(b) require any person of a prescribed description to provide any information or evidence of a prescribed description which the Board consider they may need for that purpose,

by the date specified in the notice.

### 16 Other revised decisions

(1) Where, at any time during the period for which an award of a tax credit is made to a person or persons, the Board have reasonable grounds for believing—

(a) that the rate at which the tax credit has been awarded to him or them for the period differs from the rate at which he is, or they are, entitled to the tax credit for the period, or

(b) that he has, or they have, ceased to be, or never been, entitled to the tax credit for the period,

the Board may decide to amend or terminate the award.

(2) Where, at any time during the period for which an award of a tax credit is made to a person or persons, the Board believe—

(a) that the rate at which a tax credit has been awarded to him or them for the period may differ from the rate at which he is, or they are, entitled to it for the period, or

(b) that he or they may have ceased to be, or never been, entitled to the tax credit for the period,

the Board may give a notice under subsection (3).

(3) A notice under this subsection may—

(a) require the person, or either or both of the persons, to whom the tax credit was awarded to provide any information or evidence which the Board consider they may need for considering whether to amend or terminate the award under subsection (1), or

(b) require any person of a prescribed description to provide any information or evidence of a prescribed description which the Board consider they may need for that purpose,

by the date specified in the notice.

## 17 Final notice

(1) Where a tax credit has been awarded for the whole or part of a tax year—

(a) for awards made on single claims, the Board must give a notice relating to the tax year to the person to whom the tax credit was awarded, and

(b) for awards made on joint claims, the Board must give such a notice to the persons to whom the tax credit was awarded (with separate copies of the notice for each of them if the Board consider appropriate).

(2) The notice must either—

(a) require that the person or persons must, by the date specified for the purposes of this subsection, declare that the relevant circumstances were as specified or state any respects in which they were not, or

(b) inform the person or persons that he or they will be treated as having declared in response to the notice that the relevant circumstances were as specified unless, by that date, he states or they state any respects in which they were not.

(3) "Relevant circumstances" means circumstances (other than income) affecting—

(a) the entitlement of the person, or joint entitlement of the persons, to the tax credit, or

(b) the amount of the tax credit to which he was entitled, or they were jointly entitled,

for the tax year.

(4) The notice must either—

(a) require that the person or persons must, by the date specified for the purposes of this subsection, declare that the amount of the current year income or estimated current year income (depending on which is specified) was the amount, or fell within the range, specified or comply with subsection (5), or

(b) inform the person or persons that he or they will be treated as having declared in response to the notice that the amount of the current year income or estimated current year income (depending on which is specified) was the amount, or fell within the range, specified unless, by that date, he complies or they comply with subsection (5).

(5) To comply with this subsection the person or persons must either—

(a) state the current year income or his or their estimate of the current year income (making clear which), or

(b) declare that, throughout the period to which the award related, subsection (1) of section 7 did not apply to him or them by virtue of subsection (2) of that section.

(6) The notice may—

(a) require that the person or persons must, by the date specified for the purposes of subsection (4), declare that the amount of the previous year income was the amount, or fell within the range, specified or comply with subsection (7), or

(b) inform the person or persons that he or they will be treated as having declared in response to the notice that the amount of the previous year income was the amount, or fell within the range, specified unless, by that date, he complies or they comply with subsection (7).

(7) To comply with this subsection the person or persons must either—

(a) state the previous year income, or

(b) make the declaration specified in subsection (5)(b).

(8) The notice must inform the person or persons that if he or they—

(a) makes or make a declaration under paragraph (a) of subsection (4), or is or are treated as making a declaration under paragraph (b) of that subsection, in relation to estimated current year income (or the range within which estimated current year income fell), or

(b) states or state under subsection (5)(a) his or their estimate of the current year income,

he or they will be treated as having declared in response to the notice that the amount of the (actual) current year income was as estimated unless, by the date specified for the purposes of this subsection, he states or they state the current year income.

(9) "Specified", in relation to a notice, means specified in the notice.

(10) Regulations may—

(a) provide that, in prescribed circumstances, one person may act for another in response to a notice under this section, and

(b) provide that, in prescribed circumstances, anything done by one member of a married couple or an unmarried couple in response to a notice given under this section is to be treated as also done by the other member of the married couple or unmarried couple.

## 18 Decisions after final notice

(1) After giving a notice under section 17 the Board must decide—

(a) whether the person was entitled, or the persons were jointly entitled, to the tax credit, and

(b) if so, the amount of the tax credit to which he was entitled, or they were jointly entitled,

for the tax year.

(2) But, subject to subsection (3), that decision must not be made before a declaration or statement has been made in response to the relevant provisions of the notice.

(3) If a declaration or statement has not been made in response to the relevant provisions of the notice on or before the date specified for the purposes of section 17(4), that decision may be made after that date.

(4) In subsections (2) and (3) "the relevant provisions of the notice" means—

(a) the provision included in the notice by virtue of subsection (2) of section 17,

(b) the provision included in the notice by virtue of subsection (4) of that section, and

(c) any provision included in the notice by virtue of subsection (6) of that section.

(5) Where the Board make a decision under subsection (1) on or before the date referred to in subsection (3), they may revise it if a new declaration or statement is made on or before that date.

(6) If the person or persons to whom a notice under section 17 is given is or are within paragraph (a) or (b) of subsection (8) of that section, the Board must decide again—

(a) whether the person was entitled, or the persons were jointly entitled, to the tax credit, and

(b) if so, the amount of the tax credit to which he was entitled, or they were jointly entitled,

for the tax year.

(7) But, subject to subsection (8), that decision must not be made before a statement has been made in response to the provision included in the notice by virtue of subsection (8) of section 17.

(8) If a statement has not been made in response to the provision included in the notice by virtue of that subsection on or before the date specified for the purposes of that subsection, that decision may be made after that date.

(9) Where the Board make a decision under subsection (6) on or before the date referred to in subsection (8), they may revise it if a new statement is made on or before that date.

(10) Before exercising a function imposed or conferred on them by subsection (1), (5), (6) or (9), the Board may by notice require the person, or either or both of the persons, to whom the notice under section 17 was given to provide any further information or evidence which the Board consider they may need for exercising the function by the date specified in the notice.

(11) Subject to sections 19 and 20 and regulations under section 21 (and to any revision under subsection (5) or (9) and any appeal)—

(a) in a case in which a decision is made under subsection (6) in relation to a person or persons and a tax credit for a tax year, that decision, and

(b) in any other case, the decision under subsection (1) in relation to a person or persons and a tax credit for a tax year,

is conclusive as to the entitlement of the person, or the joint entitlement of the persons, to the tax credit for the tax year and the amount of the tax credit to which he was entitled, or they were jointly entitled, for the tax year.

## 19 Power to enquire

(1) The Board may enquire into—

(a) the entitlement of a person, or the joint entitlement of persons, to a tax credit for a tax year, and

(b) the amount of the tax credit to which he was entitled, or they were jointly entitled, for the tax year,

if they give notice to the person, or each of the persons, during the period allowed for the initiation of an enquiry.

(2) As part of the enquiry the Board may by notice—

(a) require the person, or either or both of the persons, to provide any information or evidence which the Board consider they may need for the purposes of the enquiry, or

(b) require any person of a prescribed description to provide any information or evidence of a prescribed description which the Board consider they may need for those purposes,

by the date specified in the notice.

(3) On an enquiry the Board must decide—

(a) whether the person was entitled, or the persons were jointly entitled, to the tax credit, and

(b) if so, the amount of the tax credit to which he was entitled, or they were jointly entitled,

for the tax year.

(4) The period allowed for the initiation of an enquiry is the period beginning immediately after the relevant section 18 decision and ending—

(a) if the person, or either of the persons, to whom the enquiry relates is required by section 8 of the Taxes Management Act 1970 (c. 9) to make a return, with the day on which the return becomes final (or, if both of the persons are so required and their returns become final on different days, with the later of those days), or

(b) in any other case, one year after the beginning of the relevant section 17 date.

(5) "The relevant section 18 decision" means—

(a) in a case in which a decision must be made under subsection (6) of section 18 in relation to the person or persons and the tax year to which the enquiry relates, that decision, and

(b) in any other case, the decision under subsection (1) of that section in relation to the person or persons and that tax year.

(6) "The relevant section 17 date" means—

(a) in a case in which a statement may be made by the person or persons in response to provision included by virtue of subsection (8) of section 17 in the notice given to him or them under that section in relation to the tax year, the date specified in the notice for the purposes of that subsection, and

(b) in any other case, the date specified for the purposes of subsection (4) of that section in the notice given to him or them under that section in relation to the tax year.

(7) A return becomes final—

(a) if it is enquired into under section 9A of the Taxes Management Act 1970 (c. 9), when the enquiries are completed (within the meaning of section 28A of that Act), or

(b) otherwise, at the end of the period specified in subsection (2) of that section in relation to the return.

(8) An enquiry is completed at the time when the Board give notice to the person or persons of their decision under subsection (3); but if the Board give notice to the persons at different times the enquiry is completed at the later of those times.

(9) The person, or either of the persons, to whom the enquiry relates may at any time before such notice is given apply for a direction that the Board must give such a notice.

(10) Such an application is to be heard and determined in the same way as an appeal against a decision under subsection (3); and the General Commissioners or Special Commissioners hearing the application must give the direction applied for unless satisfied that the Board have reasonable grounds for not making the decision or giving the notice.

(11) Where the entitlement of a person, or the joint entitlement of persons, to a tax credit for a tax year has been enquired into under this section, it is not to be the subject of a further notice under subsection (1).

(12) Subject to section 20 and regulations under section 21 (and to any appeal), a decision under subsection (3) in relation to a person or persons and a tax credit for a tax year is conclusive as to the entitlement of the person, or the joint entitlement of the persons, to the tax credit for the tax year and the amount of the tax credit to which he was entitled, or they were jointly entitled, for the tax year.

**20 Decisions on discovery**

(1) Where in consequence of a person's income tax liability being revised the Board have reasonable grounds for believing that a conclusive decision relating to his entitlement to a tax credit for a tax year (whether or not jointly with another person) is not correct, the Board may decide to revise that decision.

(2) A person's income tax liability is revised—

(a) on the taking effect of an amendment of a return of his under section 9ZA(1) of the Taxes Management Act 1970,

(b) on the issue of a notice of correction under section 9ZB of that Act amending a return of his (provided that he does not give a notice of rejection before the end of the period of thirty days beginning with the date of issue of the notice of correction),

(c) on the amendment of an assessment of his by notice under section 9C of that Act,

(d) on the amendment of a return of his under section 12ABA(3)(a) of that Act,

(e) on the amendment of a return of his under subsection (6)(a) of section 12ABB of that Act after the correction of a partnership return under that section (provided that the amendment does not cease to have effect by reason of the rejection of the correction under subsection (4) of that section),

(f) on the issue of a closure notice under section 28A of that Act making amendments of a return of his,

(g) on the amendment of a return of his under section 28B(4)(a) of that Act,

(h) on the making of an assessment as regards him under section 29(1) of that Act,

(i) on the vacation of the whole or part of an assessment of his under section 32 of that Act,

(j) on giving him relief under section 33 of that Act, or

(k) on the determination (or settlement) of an appeal against the making, amendment or vacation of an assessment or return, or a decision on a claim for relief, under any of the provisions mentioned in paragraphs (c), (f) and (h) to (j).

(3) But no decision may be made under subsection (1)—

(a) unless it is too late to enquire into the person's entitlement under section 19, or

(b) after the period of one year beginning when the person's income tax liability is revised.

(4) Where the Board have reasonable grounds for believing that—

(a) a conclusive decision relating to the entitlement of a person, or the joint entitlement of persons, to a tax credit for a tax year is not correct, and

(b) that is attributable to fraud or neglect on the part of the person, or of either of the persons, or on the part of any person acting for him, or either of them,

the Board may decide to revise that decision.

(5) But no decision may be made under subsection (4)—

(a) unless it is too late to enquire into the entitlement, or joint entitlement, under section 19, or

(b) after the period of five years beginning with the end of the tax year to which the conclusive decision relates.

(6) "Conclusive decision", in relation to the entitlement of a person, or joint entitlement of persons, to a tax credit for a tax year, means—

(a) a decision in relation to it under section 18(1), (5), (6) or (9) or 19(3) or a previous decision under this section, or

(b) a decision under regulations under section 21 relating to a decision within paragraph (a),

including a decision made on an appeal against such a decision.

(7) Subject to any subsequent decision under this section and to regulations under section 21 (and to any appeal), a decision under subsection (1) or (4) in relation to a person or persons and a tax credit for a tax year is conclusive as to the entitlement of the person, or the joint entitlement of the persons, to the tax credit for the tax year and the amount of the tax credit to which he was entitled, or they were jointly entitled, for the tax year.

### 21 Decisions subject to official error

Regulations may make provision for a decision under section 14(1), 15(1), 16(1), 18(1), (5), (6) or (9), 19(3) or 20(1) or (4) to be revised in favour of the person or persons to whom it relates if it is incorrect by reason of official error (as defined by the regulations).

### 22 Information etc. requirements: supplementary

(1) Regulations may make provision as to the manner and form in which—

(a) information or evidence is to be provided in compliance with a requirement imposed by a notice under section 14(2), 15(2), 16(3), 18(10) or 19(2), or

(b) a declaration or statement is to be made in response to a notice under section 17.

(2) Regulations may make provision as to the dates which may be specified in a notice under section 14(2), 15(2), 16(3), 17, 18(10) or 19(2).

## 23 Notice of decisions

(1) When a decision is made under section 14(1), 15(1), 16(1), 18(1), (5), (6) or (9), 19(3) or 20(1) or (4) or regulations under section 21, the Board must give notice of the decision to the person, or each of the persons, to whom it relates.

(2) Notice of a decision must state the date on which it is given and include details of any right to appeal against the decision under section 38.

(3) Notice need not be given of a decision made under section 14(1) or 18(1) or (6) on the basis of declarations made or treated as made by the person or persons in response to the notice given to him or them under section 17 if—

(a) that notice, or

(b) in the case of a decision under subsection (6) of section 18, that notice or the notice of the decision under subsection (1) of that section,

stated what the decision would be and the date on which it would be made.

*Payment*

## 24 Payments

(1) Where the Board have made an award of a tax credit, the amount of the tax credit awarded must be paid to the person to whom the award is made, subject to subsections (2) and (3).

(2) Where an award of a tax credit is made to the members of a married couple or an unmarried couple, payments of the tax credit, or of any element of the tax credit, are to be made to whichever of them is prescribed.

(3) Where an award of a tax credit is made on a claim which was made by one person on behalf of another, payments of the tax credit, or of any element of the tax credit, are to be made to whichever of those persons is prescribed.

(4) Where an award of a tax credit has been made to a person or persons for the whole or part of a tax year, payments may, in prescribed circumstances, continue to be made for any period, after the tax year, within which he is or they are entitled to make a claim for the tax credit for the next tax year.

(5) Payments made under subsection (4) are to be treated for the purposes of this section and the following provisions of this Part as if they were payments of the tax credit for the next tax year.

(6) Subject to section 25, payments of a tax credit must be made by the Board.

(7) Regulations may make provision about the time when and the manner in which a tax credit, or any element of a tax credit, is to be paid by the Board.

(8) If the regulations make provision for payments of a tax credit, or any element of a tax credit, to be made by the Board by way of a credit to a bank account or other account notified to the Board, the regulations may provide that entitlement to the tax credit or element is dependent on an account having been notified to the Board in accordance with the regulations.

## 25 Payments of working tax credit by employers

(1) Regulations may require employers, when making Schedule E payments and in any such other circumstances as may be prescribed, to pay working tax credit, or prescribed elements of working tax credit, to employees.

(2) The regulations may, in particular, include provision—

(a) requiring employers to make payments of working tax credit, or prescribed elements of working tax credit, in accordance with notices given to them by the Board,

(b) for the payment by the Board of working tax credit in cases where an employer does not make payments of working tax credit, or prescribed elements of working tax credit, in accordance with the regulations and with any notices given by the Board,

(c) prescribing circumstances in which employers are not required to make, or to continue making, payments of working tax credit, or prescribed elements of working tax credit,

(d) for the provision of information or evidence for the purpose of enabling the Board to be satisfied whether employers are complying with notices given by the Board and with the regulations,

(e) requiring employers to provide information to employees (in their itemised pay statements or otherwise),

(f) for the funding by the Board of working tax credit paid or to be paid by employers (whether by way of set off against income tax, national insurance contributions or student loan deductions for which they are accountable to the Board or otherwise),

(g) for the recovery by the Board from an employer of funding under paragraph (f) to the extent that it exceeds the amount of working tax credit paid by the employer,

(h) for the payment of interest at the prescribed rate on sums due from or to the Board, and for determining the date from which interest is to be calculated, and

(i) for appeals with respect to matters arising under the regulations which would otherwise not be the subject of an appeal.

(3) Section 20 of the Taxes Management Act 1970 (c. 9) (power to call for documents etc.) applies (with sections 20B and 20BB) in relation to an employer's compliance with regulations under this section as in relation to a person's tax liability (but subject to the modifications provided by subsection (4)).

(4) Those sections apply by virtue of subsection (3) as if—

(a) the references to the taxpayer, a taxpayer or a class of taxpayers were to the employer, an employer or a class of employers,

(b) the reference to any provision of the Taxes Acts were to regulations under this section,

(c) the references to the proper assessment or collection of tax were to the proper award or payment of working tax credit,

(d) the reference to an appeal relating to tax were to an appeal relating to compliance with regulations under this section, and

(e) the reference to believing that tax has been, or may have been, lost to the Crown were to believing that the Crown has, or may have, incurred a loss.

(5) In this Part—

"employee" means a person who receives any Schedule E payment, and

"employer", in relation to an employee, means a person who makes any such payment to the employee.

(6) "Schedule E payment" means a payment of, or on account of, any income assessable to income tax under Schedule E.

(7) "Student loan deductions" means deductions in accordance with regulations under section 22(5) of the Teaching and Higher Education Act 1998 (c. 30), section 73B(3) of the Education (Scotland) Act 1980 (c. 44) or Article 3(5) of the Education (Student Support) (Northern Ireland) Order 1998 (S.I. 1998/1760 (N.I. 14)).

### 26 Liability of officers for sums paid to employers

(1) Regulations may provide that where—

(a) an employer which is a body corporate has failed to repay any funding to the Board in accordance with regulations made under section 25(2)(g), and

(b) the provision of the funding, or the failure by the employer to repay the funding, appears to the Board to be attributable to fraud or neglect on the part of one or more individuals who, at the time of the fraud or neglect, were officers of the body corporate ("culpable officers"),

the culpable officers are required to pay to the Board the amount of funding recoverable by the Board from the employer.

(2) Regulations under this section must include provision—

(a) for any amount paid to the Board by a culpable officer in accordance with the regulations to be deducted from the amount of funding liable to be repaid by the employer,

(b) for the amount which a culpable officer is liable to pay under the regulations to be reduced where the amount of funding recoverable from the employer is reduced by payments made to the Board by the employer, and

(c) for the Board to repay to a culpable officer the amount (if any) by which the amount that he has paid to the Board pursuant to the regulations exceeds the reduced amount that he is liable to pay by virtue of paragraph (b).

(3) Regulations under this section may include provision—

(a) requiring payments by culpable officers to be made in accordance with notices given to them by the Board,

(b) for determining, in cases of an employer in relation to which there is more than one culpable officer, the proportion of the amount of funding recoverable from the employer that is payable by each culpable officer,

(c) for the payment of interest at the prescribed rate on sums due to or from the Board, and for determining the date from which interest is to be calculated, and

(d) for appeals with respect to matters arising under the regulations.

(4) "Officer", in relation to a body corporate, means—

(a) any director, manager, secretary or other similar officer of the body corporate, or any person purporting to act as such, and

(b) in a case where the affairs of the body corporate are managed by its members, any member of the body corporate exercising functions of management with respect to it or purporting to do so.

## 27 Rights of employees

Schedule 1 (rights of employees not to suffer unfair dismissal or other detriment) has effect.

## 28 Overpayments

(1) Where the amount of a tax credit paid for a tax year to a person or persons exceeds the amount of the tax credit to which he is entitled, or they are jointly entitled, for the tax year (as determined in accordance with the provision made by and by virtue of sections 18 to 21), the Board may decide that the excess, or any part of it, is to be repaid to the Board.

(2) In this Part such an excess is referred to as an overpayment.

(3) For overpayments made under awards on single claims, the person to whom the tax credit was awarded is liable to repay the amount which the Board decide is to be repaid.

(4) For overpayments made under awards on joint claims, the persons to whom the tax credit was awarded are jointly and severally liable to repay the amount which the Board decide is to be repaid unless the Board decide that each is to repay a specified part of that amount.

(5) Where it appears to the Board that there is likely to be an overpayment of a tax credit for a tax year under an award made to a person or persons, the Board may, with a view to reducing or eliminating the overpayment, amend the award or any other award of any tax credit made to the person or persons; but this subsection does not apply once a decision is taken in relation to the person or persons for the tax year under section 18(1).

(6) Where the Board decide under section 16 to terminate an award of a tax credit made to a person or persons on the ground that at no time during the period to which the award related did the person or persons satisfy—

(a) section 8(1) (if the award related to child tax credit), or

(b) section 10(1) (if it related to working tax credit),

the Board may decide that the amount paid under the award, or any part of it, is to be treated for the purposes of this Part (apart from subsection (5)) as an overpayment.

## 29 Recovery of overpayments

(1) Where an amount is liable to be repaid by a person or persons under section 28, the Board must give him, or each of them, a notice specifying the amount.

(2) The notice must state which of subsections (3) to (5) is to apply in relation to the amount or any specified part of the amount; and a notice may at any time be replaced by another notice containing a different statement.

(3) Where a notice states that this subsection applies in relation to an amount (or part of an amount), it is to be treated for the purposes of Part 6 of the Taxes Management Act 1970 (c. 9) (collection and recovery) as if it were tax charged in an assessment and due and payable by the person or persons to whom the notice was given at the end of the period of thirty days beginning with the day on which the notice is given.

(4) Where a notice states that this subsection applies in relation to an amount (or part of an amount), it may, subject to provision made by regulations, be recovered by deduction from payments of any tax credit under an award made for any period to the person, or either or both of the persons, to whom the notice was given.

(5) Where a notice states that this subsection applies in relation to an amount (or part of an amount), regulations under section 203(2)(a) of the Income and Corporation Taxes Act 1988 (c. 1) (PAYE) apply to it as if it were an underpayment of tax for a previous year of assessment by the person or persons to whom the notice was given.

### 30 Underpayments

(1) Where it has been determined in accordance with the provision made by and by virtue of sections 18 to 21 that a person was entitled, or persons were jointly entitled, to a tax credit for a tax year and either—

(a) the amount of the tax credit paid to him or them for that tax year was less than the amount of the tax credit to which it was so determined that he is entitled or they are jointly entitled, or

(b) no payment of the tax credit was made to him or them for that tax year,

the amount of the difference, or of his entitlement or their joint entitlement, must be paid to him or to whichever of them is prescribed.

(2) Where the claim for the tax credit was made by one person on behalf of another, the payment is to be made to whichever of those persons is prescribed.

*Penalties*

### 31 Incorrect statements etc.

(1) Where a person fraudulently or negligently—

(a) makes an incorrect statement or declaration in or in connection with a claim for a tax credit or a notification of a change of circumstances given in accordance with regulations under section 6 or in response to a notice under section 17, or

(b) gives incorrect information or evidence in response to a requirement imposed on him by virtue of section 14(2), 15(2), 16(3), 18(10) or 19(2) or regulations under section 25,

a penalty not exceeding £3,000 may be imposed on him.

(2) Where a person liable to a penalty under subsection (1) is a person making, or who has made, a claim for a tax credit for a period jointly with another and the penalty is imposed—

(a) under paragraph (a) of that subsection in respect of the claim, a notification relating to the tax credit claimed or a notice relating to the tax credit awarded on the claim, or

(b) under paragraph (b) of that subsection in respect of a requirement imposed on him with respect to the tax credit for the period,

a penalty of an amount not exceeding £3,000 may be imposed on the other person unless subsection (3) applies.

(3) This subsection applies if the other person was not, and could not reasonably have been expected to have been, aware that the person liable to the penalty under subsection (1) had fraudulently or negligently made the incorrect statement or declaration or given the incorrect information or evidence.

(4) Where penalties are imposed under subsections (1) and (2) in respect of the same statement, declaration, information or evidence, their aggregate amount must not exceed £3,000.

(5) Where a person acts for another—

(a) in or in connection with a claim or notification referred to in subsection (1), or

(b) in response to a notice so referred to,

subsection (1) applies to him (as well as to any person to whom it applies apart from this subsection).

### 32 Failure to comply with requirements

(1) Where a person fails—

(a) to provide any information or evidence which he is required to provide by virtue of section 14(2), 15(2), 16(3), 18(10) or 19(2) or regulations under section 25, or

(b) to comply with a requirement imposed on him by a notice under section 17 by virtue of subsection (2)(a), (4)(a) or (6)(a) of that section,

the penalties specified in subsection (2) may be imposed on him.

(2) The penalties are—

(a) a penalty not exceeding £300, and

(b) if the failure continues after a penalty is imposed under paragraph (a), a further penalty or penalties not exceeding £60 for each day on which the failure continues after the day on which the penalty under that paragraph was imposed (but excluding any day for which a penalty under this paragraph has already been imposed).

(3) Where a person fails to give a notification required by regulations under section 6(3), a penalty not exceeding £300 may be imposed on him.

(4) No penalty under subsection (2) may be imposed on a person in respect of a failure after the failure has been remedied.

(5) For the purposes of this section a person is to be taken not to have failed to provide information or evidence, comply with a requirement or give a notification which must be provided, complied with or given by a particular time—

(a) if he provided, complied with or gave it within such further time (if any) as the Board may have allowed,

(b) if he had a reasonable excuse for not providing, complying with or giving it by that time, or

(c) if, after having had such an excuse, he provided, complied with or gave it without unreasonable delay.

(6) Where the members of a married couple or an unmarried couple both fail as mentioned in subsection (1)(b), the aggregate amount of any penalties under subsection (2) imposed on them in relation to their failures must not exceed the amounts specified in that subsection; and where the members of a married couple or an unmarried couple both fail as mentioned in subsection (3), the aggregate amount of any penalties imposed on them in relation to their failures must not exceed £300.

### 33 Failure by employers to make correct payments

(1) Where an employer refuses or repeatedly fails to make to an employee payments of tax credits which he is required to make to him by regulations under section 25 and, as a result, the Board make payments to the employee in accordance with regulations under subsection (2)(b) of that section, a penalty not exceeding £3,000 may be imposed on the employer.

(2) Where an employer has, by reason of his fraud or neglect, not paid to an employee for a tax year the correct amount of any tax credit which he is required by regulations under section 25 to pay to him for that tax year, a penalty not exceeding £3,000 may be imposed on the employer.

(3) But no penalty may be imposed on an employer under subsection (2) in respect of payments which are incorrect only because of a refusal or failure in respect of which a penalty is imposed on him under subsection (1).

### 34 Supplementary

Schedule 2 (penalties: supplementary) has effect.

*Fraud*

### 35 Offence of fraud

(1) A person commits an offence if he is knowingly concerned in any fraudulent activity undertaken with a view to obtaining payments of a tax credit by him or any other person.

(2) A person who commits an offence under subsection (1) is liable—

(a) on summary conviction, to imprisonment for a term not exceeding six months, or a fine not exceeding the statutory maximum, or both, or

(b) on conviction on indictment, to imprisonment for a term not exceeding seven years, or a fine, or both.

### 36 Powers in relation to documents

(1) Section 20BA of the Taxes Management Act 1970 (c. 9) (orders for delivery of documents) applies (with Schedule 1AA and section 20BB) in relation to offences

involving fraud in connection with, or in relation to, tax credits as in relation to offences involving serious fraud in connection with, or in relation to, tax.

(2) Section 20C (entry with warrant to obtain documents) of that Act applies (with section 20CC) in relation to offences involving serious fraud in connection with, or in relation to, tax credits as in relation to offences involving serious fraud in connection with, or in relation to, tax (but subject to the modification provided by subsection (3)).

(3) Subsection (1A) of section 20C applies by virtue of subsection (2) as if the references to the proper assessment or collection of tax were to the proper award or payment of a tax credit.

(4) Any regulations under Schedule 1AA to the Taxes Management Act 1970 which are in force immediately before the commencement of subsection (1) apply, subject to any necessary modifications, for the purposes of that Schedule as they apply by virtue of that subsection (until amended or revoked).

*Interest*

## 37 Interest

(1) If an overpayment of a tax credit for a period is attributable to fraud or neglect on the part of the person, or either or both of the persons, to whom the award of the tax credit was made (or a person acting for him, or for either or both of them, in making the claim for the tax credit), the Board may decide that the whole or any part of the overpayment is to carry interest.

(2) Where the Board so decide the overpayment (or part of the overpayment) carries interest at a prescribed rate from the date thirty days after the appropriate date.

(3) "The appropriate date" is—

(a) in the case of an amount treated as an overpayment by virtue of section 28(6), the date of the decision under section 16 to terminate the award, and

(b) in any other case, the date specified for the purposes of subsection (4) of section 17 in the notice given to the person or persons under that section in relation to the tax credit.

(4) The Board must give notice of a decision under subsection (1) to the person, or each of the persons, to whom it relates; and the notice must state the date on which it is given and include details of the right to appeal against the decision under section 38.

(5) A penalty under any of sections 31 to 33 carries interest at the prescribed rate from the date on which it becomes due and payable; but the Board may in their discretion mitigate any interest or entirely remit any interest which would otherwise be carried by a penalty.

(6) Any interest carried under this section by an overpayment or penalty is to be regarded for the purposes of section 29(3) to (5) or paragraph 7 of Schedule 2 as if it were part of the overpayment or penalty.

*Appeals*

## 38 Appeals

(1) An appeal may be brought against—

(a) a decision under section 14(1), 15(1), 16(1), 19(3) or 20(1) or (4) or regulations under section 21,

(b) the relevant section 18 decision in relation to a person or persons and a tax credit for a tax year and any revision of that decision under that section,

(c) a determination of a penalty under paragraph 1 of Schedule 2, and

(d) a decision under section 37(1).

(2) "The relevant section 18 decision" means—

(a) in a case in which a decision must be made under subsection (6) of section 18 in relation to the person or persons and the tax credit for the tax year, that decision, and

(b) in any other case, the decision under subsection (1) of that section in relation to the person or persons and the tax credit for the tax year.

## 39 Exercise of right of appeal

(1) Notice of an appeal under section 38 against a decision must be given to the Board in the prescribed manner within the period of thirty days after the date on which notice of the decision was given (or, in the case of a decision to which section 23(3) applies, the date of the decision).

(2) Notice of such an appeal must specify the grounds of appeal.

(3) An appeal under section 38 is to the General Commissioners but the appellant may elect (in accordance with section 46(1) of the Taxes Management Act 1970 (c. 9)) to bring the appeal before the Special Commissioners instead.

(4) Subsections (2) to (7) of section 31D of the Taxes Management Act 1970 (which relate to an election to bring proceedings before the Special Commissioners) have effect in relation to an election under subsection (3) (as in relation to an election under subsection (1) of that section).

(5) On the hearing of an appeal under section 38 the General Commissioners or Special Commissioners may allow the appellant to put forward grounds not specified in the notice, and take them into consideration if satisfied that the omission was not wilful or unreasonable.

(6) Part 5 of the Taxes Management Act 1970 (appeals to Commissioners) applies in relation to appeals under section 38 (as in relation to appeals under the Taxes Acts, within the meaning of that Act), but subject to such modifications as are prescribed.

(7) Any regulations under section 56B of the Taxes Management Act 1970 (c. 9) which are in force immediately before the commencement of subsection (6) apply, subject to any necessary modifications, for the purposes of appeals under section 38 (until amended or revoked).

*Supplementary*

### 40 Annual reports

(1) The Board must make to the Treasury an annual report about—

(a) the matters required by section 2(5) to be set forth in the accounts mentioned in section 13 of the Inland Revenue Regulation Act 1890 (c. 21),

(b) the number of awards of child tax credit and of working tax credit,

(c) the number of enquiries conducted under section 19,

(d) the number of penalties imposed under this Part, and

(e) the number of prosecutions and convictions for offences connected with tax credits.

(2) The Treasury must publish each annual report made to it under subsection (1) and lay a copy before each House of Parliament.

### 41 Annual review

(1) The Treasury must, in each tax year, review the amounts specified in subsection (2) in order to determine whether they have retained their value in relation to the general level of prices in the United Kingdom as estimated by the Treasury in such manner as it considers appropriate.

(2) The amounts are monetary amounts prescribed—

(a) under subsection (1)(a) of section 7,

(b) for the purposes of any of paragraphs (a) to (d) of subsection (3) of that section,

(c) under section 9,

(d) under section 11, otherwise than by virtue of section 12, or

(e) under subsection (2) of section 13, otherwise than by virtue of subsection (3) of that section.

(3) The Treasury must prepare a report of each review.

(4) The report must include a statement of what each amount would be if it had fully retained its value.

(5) The Treasury must publish the report and lay a copy of it before each House of Parliament.

### 42 Persons subject to immigration control

(1) Regulations may make provision in relation to persons subject to immigration control or in relation to prescribed descriptions of such persons—

(a) for excluding entitlement to, or to a prescribed element of, child tax credit or working tax credit (or both), or

(b) for this Part to apply subject to other prescribed modifications.

(2) "Person subject to immigration control" has the same meaning as in section 115 of the Immigration and Asylum Act 1999 (c. 33).

## 43 Polygamous marriages

(1) Regulations may make provision for this Part to apply in relation to persons who are parties to polygamous marriages subject to prescribed modifications.

(2) A person is a party to a polygamous marriage if—

(a) he is a party to a marriage entered into under a law which permits polygamy, and

(b) either party to the marriage has a spouse additional to the other party.

## 44 Crown employment

This Part applies in relation to persons employed by or under the Crown (as in relation to other employees).

## 45 Inalienability

(1) Every assignment of or charge on a tax credit, and every agreement to assign or charge a tax credit, is void; and, on the bankruptcy of a person entitled to a tax credit, the entitlement to the tax credit does not pass to any trustee or other person acting on behalf of his creditors.

(2) In the application of subsection (1) to Scotland—

(a) the reference to assignment is to assignation ("assign" being construed accordingly), and

(b) the reference to the bankruptcy of a person is to the sequestration of his estate or the appointment on his estate of a judicial factor under section 41 of the Solicitors (Scotland) Act 1980 (c. 46).

## 46 Giving of notices by Board

The Board may give any notice which they are required or permitted to give under this Part in any manner and form which the Board consider appropriate in the circumstances.

## 47 Consequential amendments

Schedule 3 (consequential amendments) has effect.

## 48 Interpretation

In this Part—

"child" has the meaning given by section 8(3),

"the current year income" has the meaning given by section 7(4),

"employee" and "employer" have the meaning given by section 25(5),

"the General Commissioners" means the Commissioners for the general purposes of the income tax appointed under section 2 of the Taxes Management Act 1970 (c. 9),

"the income threshold" has the meaning given by section 7(1)(a),

"joint claim" has the meaning given by section 3(8),

"married couple" has the meaning given by section 3(5),

"overpayment" has the meaning given by section 28(2) and (6),

"the previous year income" has the meaning given by section 7(5),

"qualifying remunerative work", and being engaged in it, have the meaning given by regulations under section 10(2),

"qualifying young person" has the meaning given by section 8(4),

"the relevant income" has the meaning given by section 7(3),

"responsible", in relation to a child or qualifying young person, has the meaning given by regulations under section 8(2) (for the purposes of child tax credit) or by regulations under section 10(4) (for the purposes of working tax credit),

"single claim" has the meaning given by section 3(8),

"the Special Commissioners" means the Commissioners for the special purposes of the Income Tax Acts appointed under section 4 of the Taxes Management Act 1970 (c. 9),

"tax year" means a period beginning with 6th April in one year and ending with 5th April in the next, and

"unmarried couple" has the meaning given by section 3(6).

## PART 2

## CHILD BENEFIT AND GUARDIAN'S ALLOWANCE

*Transfer of functions etc.*

### 49 Functions transferred to Treasury

(1) The functions of the Secretary of State under—

- (a) section 77 of the Social Security Contributions and Benefits Act 1992 (c. 4) (guardian's allowance: Great Britain),
- (b) Part 9 of that Act (child benefit: Great Britain), except section 142(1)(c) and (2) and paragraphs 5 and 6(1) of Schedule 10,
- (c) section 80 of the Social Security Administration Act 1992 (c. 5) (overlap with benefits under legislation of other member States: Great Britain), and
- (d) section 72 of the Social Security Act 1998 (c. 14) (power to reduce child benefit for lone parents: Great Britain),

are transferred to the Treasury.

(2) The functions of the Northern Ireland Department under—

- (a) section 77 of the Social Security Contributions and Benefits (Northern Ireland) Act 1992 (c. 7) (guardian's allowance: Northern Ireland),
- (b) Part 9 of that Act (child benefit: Northern Ireland), except section 138(1)(c) and (2) and paragraphs 5 and 6(1) of Schedule 10,
- (c) section 76 of the Social Security Administration (Northern Ireland) Act 1992 (c. 8) (overlap with benefits under legislation of other member States: Northern Ireland), and
- (d) Article 68 of the Social Security (Northern Ireland) Order 1998 (1998/1506 (N.I. 10)) (power to reduce child benefit for lone parents: Northern Ireland),

are transferred to the Treasury.

(3) The functions of the Secretary of State under Part 10 of the Social Security Administration Act 1992 (c. 5) (review and alteration of benefits: Great Britain) so far as relating to child benefit and guardian's allowance are transferred to the Treasury.

(4) The functions of the Northern Ireland Department under sections 132 to 134 of the Social Security Administration (Northern Ireland) Act 1992 (c. 8) (review and alteration of benefits: Northern Ireland) so far as relating to child benefit and guardian's allowance are transferred to the Treasury.

## 50 Functions transferred to Board

(1) The functions of the Secretary of State and the Northern Ireland Department under the provisions specified in subsection (2), so far as relating to child benefit and guardian's allowance, are transferred to the Board.

(2) The provisions referred to in subsection (1) are—

- (a) the Social Security Contributions and Benefits Act 1992 (c. 4),
- (b) the Social Security Administration Act 1992, except Part 13 (advisory bodies and consultation: Great Britain),
- (c) the Social Security Contributions and Benefits (Northern Ireland) Act 1992 (c. 7),
- (d) the Social Security Administration (Northern Ireland) Act 1992, except Part 12 (advisory bodies and consultation: Northern Ireland),
- (e) Chapter 2 of Part 1 of the Social Security Act 1998 (c. 14) (social security decisions and appeals: Great Britain),
- (f) Chapter 2 of Part 2 of the Social Security (Northern Ireland) Order 1998 (1998/1506 (N.I. 10)) (social security decisions and appeals: Northern Ireland), and
- (g) any subordinate legislation made under any of the provisions specified in section 49 or any of the preceding provisions of this subsection.

(3) This section has effect subject to section 49.

## 51 Consequential amendments

Schedule 4 (amendments consequential on transfer of functions made by sections 49 and 50) has effect.

## 52 Transfer of property, rights and liabilities

(1) This subsection transfers to and vests in the Treasury the property, rights and liabilities to which the Secretary of State or the Northern Ireland Department is entitled or subject in connection with functions transferred to the Treasury by section 49 immediately before they are transferred.

(2) This subsection transfers to and vests in the Board the property, rights and liabilities to which the Secretary of State or the Northern Ireland Department is entitled or subject in connection with functions transferred to the Board by section 50 immediately before they are transferred.

(3) A certificate given by the Treasury that any property has been transferred by subsection (1) is conclusive evidence of the transfer; and a certificate given by the

Board that any property has been transferred by subsection (2) is conclusive evidence of the transfer.

(4) Subsections (1) and (2) have effect in relation to property, rights and liabilities in spite of any provision (of whatever nature) which would prevent or restrict transfer otherwise than by this section.

(5) Subsections (1) and (2) do not apply to contracts within subsection (6); but any term of such a contract about the provision of goods or services to the Secretary of State (or a government department) or the Northern Ireland Department is to be taken to refer also to the Board in connection with any function transferred by section 49 or 50.

(6) The contracts within this subsection are contracts for the supply of goods or services to the Secretary of State or the Northern Ireland Department—

(a) which relate partly to functions transferred by section 49 or 50 and partly to other functions, or

(b) the terms of which are wholly or partly determined by a contract within paragraph (a).

(7) Her Majesty may by Order in Council make such provision for the transfer to Her Majesty's Home Civil Service of persons employed in the Northern Ireland Civil Service as appears to Her Majesty to be appropriate in consequence of the transfer of functions made by sections 49 and 50.

## 53 General functions of Board

(1) Child benefit and guardian's allowance are to be under the care and management of the Board.

(2) For the purposes of the Inland Revenue Regulation Act 1890 (c. 21) the definition of "inland revenue" in section 39 of that Act is to be taken to include child benefit and guardian's allowance.

(3) The reference in section 4(1) of that Act (appointment of collectors, officers and other persons) to collecting, receiving, managing and accounting for inland revenue is to be taken to include a reference to paying and managing child benefit and guardian's allowance.

(4) The duties of the Board under section 13 of that Act (Board to keep accounts) are to include a duty to set forth in the accounts mentioned in that section—

(a) the amounts of the several payments made by them of or in respect of child benefit and guardian's allowance,

(b) the amounts of the expenses of paying and managing child benefit and guardian's allowance, and

(c) the amounts received by them in respect of child benefit and guardian's allowance,

distinguishing in each case between amounts relating to child benefit and amounts relating to guardian's allowance.

(5) In any declaration for the purposes of section 6 of the Taxes Management Act 1970 (c. 9) (declarations on taking office), whether made before or after the commencement of this section, the reference to an offence relating to inland revenue is to be taken to include a reference to an offence relating to child benefit or guardian's allowance.

### 54 Transitional provisions

(1) Any function covered by section 49 which is a function of making subordinate legislation may be exercised by the Treasury at any time after the passing of this Act if the subordinate legislation made in the exercise of the function comes into force after the commencement of that section.

(2) Any function covered by section 50 which is a function of making subordinate legislation may be exercised by the Board at any time after the passing of this Act if the subordinate legislation made in the exercise of the function comes into force after the commencement of that section.

(3) Nothing in section 49 or 50 affects the validity of anything done by or in relation to the Secretary of State or the Northern Ireland Department before its commencement.

(4) Anything (including legal proceedings) relating to any functions transferred by section 49, or any property, rights or liabilities transferred by section 52(1), which is in the course of being done or carried on by or in relation to the Secretary of State or the Northern Ireland Department immediately before the transfer may be continued by or in relation to the Treasury.

(5) Anything (including legal proceedings) relating to any functions transferred by section 50, or any property, rights or liabilities transferred by section 52(2), which is in the course of being done or carried on by or in relation to the Secretary of State or the Northern Ireland Department immediately before the transfer may be continued by or in relation to the Board.

(6) Anything done by the Secretary of State or the Northern Ireland Department for the purposes of or in connection with any functions transferred by section 49, or any property, rights or liabilities transferred by section 52(1), which is in effect immediately before the transfer has effect afterwards as if done by the Treasury.

(7) Anything done by the Secretary of State or the Northern Ireland Department for the purposes of or in connection with any functions transferred by section 50, or any property, rights or liabilities transferred by section 52(2), which is in effect immediately before the transfer has effect afterwards as if done by the Board.

(8) The Treasury is substituted for the Secretary of State or the Northern Ireland Department in any subordinate legislation, any contracts or other documents and any legal proceedings relating to any functions transferred by section 49, or any property, rights or liabilities transferred by section 52(1), made or commenced before the transfer.

(9) The Board are substituted for the Secretary of State or the Northern Ireland Department in any subordinate legislation, any contracts or other documents and any legal proceedings relating to any functions transferred by section 50, or any property, rights or liabilities transferred by section 52(2), made or commenced before the transfer.

(10) Any order made under section 8 of the Electronic Communications Act 2000 (c. 7) which—

(a) modifies provisions relating to child benefit or guardian's allowance, and

(b) is in force immediately before the commencement of this subsection,

is to continue to have effect for the purposes of child benefit and guardian's allowance, despite subsection (7) of that section, until regulations made by the Board under section 132 of the Finance Act 1999 (c. 16) which are expressed to supersede that order come into force.

*Minor amendments*

**55 Continuing entitlement after death of child**

(1) Insert the section set out in subsection (2)—

(a) in the Social Security Contributions and Benefits Act 1992 (c. 4) after section 145 (as section 145A), and

(b) in the Social Security Contributions and Benefits (Northern Ireland) Act 1992 (c. 7) after section 141 (as section 141A).

(2) The section is—

**Entitlement after death of child**

(1) If a child dies and a person is entitled to child benefit in respect of him for the week in which his death occurs, that person shall be entitled to child benefit in respect of the child for a prescribed period following that week.

(2) If the person entitled to child benefit under subsection (1) dies before the end of that prescribed period and, at the time of his death, was—

(a) a member of a married couple and living with the person to whom he was married, or

(b) a member of an unmarried couple,

that other member of the married couple or unmarried couple shall be entitled to child benefit for the period for which the dead person would have been entitled to child benefit under subsection (1) above but for his death.

(3) If a child dies before the end of the week in which he is born, subsections (1) and (2) apply in his case as if references to the person entitled to child benefit in respect of a child for the week in which his death occurs were to the person who would have been so entitled if the child had been alive at the beginning of that week (and if any conditions which were satisfied, and any facts which existed, at the time of his death were satisfied or existed then).

(4) Where a person is entitled to child benefit in respect of a child under this section, section 77 applies with the omission of subsections (4) to (6).

(5) In this section—

"married couple" means a man and a woman who are married to each other and are neither—

(a) separated under a court order, nor

(b) separated in circumstances in which the separation is likely to be permanent, and

"unmarried couple" means a man and a woman who are not a married couple but are living together as husband and wife."

**56 Presence in United Kingdom**

(1) For section 146 of the Social Security Contributions and Benefits Act 1992 (c. 4) (persons outside Great Britain) substitute—

**"146 Presence in Great Britain**

(1) No child benefit shall be payable in respect of a child for a week unless he is in Great Britain in that week.

(2) No person shall be entitled to child benefit for a week unless he is in Great Britain in that week.

(3) Circumstances may be prescribed in which a child or other person is to be treated for the purposes of this section as being, or as not being, in Great Britain."

(2) For section 142 of the Social Security Contributions and Benefits (Northern Ireland) Act 1992 (c. 7) (persons outside Northern Ireland) substitute—

**"142 Presence in Northern Ireland**

(1) No child benefit shall be payable in respect of a child for a week unless he is in Northern Ireland in that week.

(2) No person shall be entitled to child benefit for a week unless he is in Northern Ireland in that week.

(3) Circumstances may be prescribed in which a child or other person is to be treated for the purposes of this section as being, or as not being, in Northern Ireland."

### 57 Abolition of exclusion of tax exempt persons

In Schedule 9 to—

(a) the Social Security Contributions and Benefits Act 1992, and

(b) the Social Security Contributions and Benefits (Northern Ireland) Act 1992,

omit paragraph 4 (person not entitled to child benefit if he or other prescribed person is exempt from tax under prescribed provisions).

## PART 3

## SUPPLEMENTARY

### *Information etc.*

### 58 Administrative arrangements

(1) This section applies where regulations under—

(a) section 4 or 6 of this Act,

(b) section 5 of the Social Security Administration Act 1992 (c. 5), or

(c) section 5 of the Social Security Administration (Northern Ireland) Act 1992 (c. 8),

permit or require a claim or notification relating to a tax credit, child benefit or guardian's allowance to be made or given to a relevant authority.

(2) Where this section applies, regulations may make provision—

(a) for information or evidence relating to tax credits, child benefit or guardian's allowance to be provided to the relevant authority (whether by persons by whom such claims and notifications are or have been made or given, by the Board or by other persons),

(b) for the giving of information or advice by a relevant authority to persons by whom such claims or notifications are or have been made or given, and

(c) for the recording, verification and holding, and the forwarding to the Board or a person providing services to the Board, of claims and notifications received by virtue of the regulations referred to in subsection (1) and information or evidence received by virtue of paragraph (a),

(3) "Relevant authority" means—

(a) the Secretary of State,

(b) the Northern Ireland Department, or

(c) a person providing services to the Secretary of State or the Northern Ireland Department.

### 59 Use and disclosure of information

Schedule 5 (use and disclosure of information) has effect.

*Other supplementary provisions*

### 60 Repeals

Schedule 6 (repeals) has effect.

### 61 Commencement

Apart from section 54(1) and (2), the preceding provisions of this Act come into force in accordance with orders made by the Treasury.

### 62 Transitional provisions and savings

(1) The Secretary of State may by order make as respects England and Wales and Scotland, and the Northern Ireland Department may by order make as respects Northern Ireland, any transitional provisions or savings which appear appropriate in connection with the commencement of the abolition of the increases referred to in section 1(3)(e).

(2) Subject to any provision made by virtue of subsection (1), the Treasury may by order make any transitional provisions or savings which appear appropriate in connection with the commencement of any provision of this Act.

### 63 Tax credits appeals etc.: temporary modifications

(1) Until such day as the Treasury may by order appoint, Part 1 of this Act has effect subject to the modifications specified in this section; and an order under this subsection may include any transitional provisions or savings which appear appropriate.

(2) Except in the case of an appeal against an employer penalty, an appeal under section 38 is to an appeal tribunal (rather than to the General Commissioners or Special Commissioners).

(3) The function of giving a direction under section 19(10) is a function of an appeal tribunal (rather than of the General Commissioners or Special Commissioners).

(4) Except in the case of an employer information penalty, proceedings under paragraph 3 of Schedule 2 are by way of information made to an appeal tribunal (rather than to the General Commissioners or Special Commissioners).

(5) So far as is appropriate in consequence of subsections (2) to (4)—

(a) the references to the General Commissioners or Special Commissioners in sections 19(10) and 39(5) and paragraphs 2 and 3(2) of Schedule 2 are to the appeal tribunal, and

(b) subsections (3) and (4) of section 39 do not apply.

(6) An appeal under paragraph 2(2) or 4(1) of Schedule 2 from a decision of, or against the determination of a penalty by, an appeal tribunal lies to a Social Security Commissioner (rather than to the High Court or Court of Session).

(7) So far as is appropriate in consequence of subsection (6), the references in paragraphs 2(2) and 4 of Schedule 2 to the High Court and the Court of Session are to the Social Security Commissioner.

(8) Regulations may apply any provision contained in—

(a) Chapter 2 of Part 1 of the Social Security Act 1998 (c. 14) (social security appeals: Great Britain),

(b) Chapter 2 of Part 2 of the Social Security (Northern Ireland) Order 1998 (S.I. 1998/1506 (N.I. 10)) (social security appeals: Northern Ireland), or

(c) section 54 of the Taxes Management Act 1970 (c. 9) (settling of appeals by agreement),

in relation to appeals which, by virtue of this section, are to an appeal tribunal or lie to a Social Security Commissioner, but subject to such modifications as are prescribed.

(9) Except in the case of appeals against employer penalties, subsections (6) and (7) of section 39 do not apply.

(10) "Appeal tribunal" means an appeal tribunal constituted—

(a) in Great Britain, under Chapter 1 of Part 1 of the Social Security Act 1998, or

(b) in Northern Ireland, under Chapter 1 of Part 2 of the Social Security (Northern Ireland) Order 1998.

(11) "Employer penalty" means—

(a) a penalty under section 31 or 32 relating to a requirement imposed by virtue of regulations under section 25, or

(b) a penalty under section 33.

(12) "Employer information penalty" means a penalty under section 32(2)(a) relating to a requirement imposed by virtue of regulations under section 25.

(13) "Social Security Commissioner" means—

(a) in Great Britain, the Chief Social Security Commissioner or any other Social Security Commissioner appointed under the Social Security Act 1998 (c. 14) or a tribunal of three or more Commissioners constituted under section 16(7) of that Act, and

(b) in Northern Ireland, the Chief Social Security Commissioner or any other Social Security Commissioner appointed under the Social Security Administration (Northern Ireland) Act 1992 (c. 8) or a tribunal of two or more Commissioners constituted under Article 16(7) of the Social Security (Northern Ireland) Order 1998 (S.I. 1998/1506 (N.I. 10)).

### 64 Northern Ireland

(1) The Northern Ireland Act 1998 (c. 47) has effect subject to the amendments in subsections (2) and (3).

(2) In Schedule 2 (excepted matters), after paragraph 10 insert—

"10A Tax credits under Part 1 of the Tax Credits Act 2002.

10B Child benefit and guardian's allowance."

(3) In section 87 (consultation and co-ordination on social security matters), after subsection (6) insert—

"(6A) But this section does not apply to the legislation referred to in subsection (6) to the extent that it relates to child benefit or guardian's allowance."

(4) For the purposes of that Act, a provision of—

(a) an Act of the Northern Ireland Assembly, or

(b) a Bill for such an Act,

which amends or repeals any of the provisions of the Employment Rights (Northern Ireland) Order 1996 (S.I. 1996/1919 (N.I. 16)) dealt with in Schedule 1 shall not be treated as dealing with tax credits if the Act or Bill deals with employment rights conferred otherwise than by that Schedule in the same way.

### 65 Regulations, orders and schemes

(1) Any power to make regulations under sections 3, 7 to 13, 42 and 43, and any power to make regulations under this Act prescribing a rate of interest, is exercisable by the Treasury.

(2) Any other power to make regulations under this Act is exercisable by the Board.

(3) Subject to subsection (4), any power to make regulations, orders or schemes under this Act is exercisable by statutory instrument.

(4) The power—

(a) of the Department of Health, Social Services and Public Safety to make schemes under section 12(5), and

(b) of the Northern Ireland Department to make orders under section 62(1),

is exercisable by statutory rule for the purposes of the Statutory Rules (Northern Ireland) Order 1979 (S.I. 1979/1573 (N.I. 12)).

(5) Regulations may not be made under section 25 or 26 in relation to appeals in Scotland without the consent of the Scottish Ministers.

(6) Regulations may not be made under section 39(6) or 63(8) without the consent of the Lord Chancellor and the Scottish Ministers.

(7) Any power to make regulations under this Act may be exercised—

(a) in relation to all cases to which it extends, to all those cases with prescribed exceptions or to prescribed cases or classes of case,

(b) so as to make as respects the cases in relation to which it is exercised the full provision to which it extends or any less provision (whether by way of exception or otherwise),

(c) so as to make the same provision for all cases in relation to which it is exercised or different provision for different cases or classes of case or different provision as respects the same case or class of case for different purposes,

(d) so as to make provision unconditionally or subject to any prescribed condition,

(e) so as to provide for a person to exercise a discretion in dealing with any matter.

(8) Any regulations made under a power under this Act to prescribe a rate of interest may—

(a) either themselves specify a rate of interest or make provision for any such rate to be determined by reference to such rate or the average of such rates as may be referred to in the regulations,

(b) provide for rates to be reduced below, or increased above, what they otherwise would be by specified amounts or by reference to specified formulae,

(c) provide for rates arrived at by reference to averages to be rounded up or down,

(d) provide for circumstances in which alteration of a rate of interest is or is not to take place, and

(e) provide that alterations of rates are to have effect for periods beginning on or after a day determined in accordance with the regulations in relation to interest running from before that day as well as from or from after that day.

(9) Any power to make regulations or a scheme under this Act includes power to make any incidental, supplementary, consequential or transitional provision which appears appropriate for the purposes of, or in connection with, the regulations or scheme.

### 66 Parliamentary etc. control of instruments

(1) No regulations to which this subsection applies may be made unless a draft of the instrument containing them (whether or not together with other provisions) has been laid before, and approved by a resolution of, each House of Parliament.

(2) Subsection (1) applies to—

(a) regulations prescribing monetary amounts that are required to be reviewed under section 41,

(b) regulations made by virtue of subsection (2) of section 12 prescribing the amount in excess of which charges are not taken into account for the purposes of that subsection, and

(c) the first regulations made under sections 7(8) and (9), 9, 11, 12 and 13(2).

(3) A statutory instrument containing—

(a) regulations under this Act,

(b) a scheme made by the Secretary of State under section 12(5), or

(c) an Order in Council under section 52(7),

is (unless a draft of the instrument has been laid before, and approved by a resolution of, each House of Parliament) subject to annulment in pursuance of a resolution of either House of Parliament.

(4) A statutory instrument containing a scheme made by the Scottish Ministers under section 12(5) is subject to annulment in pursuance of a resolution of the Scottish Parliament.

(5) A statutory rule containing a scheme made by the Department of Health, Social Services and Public Safety under section 12(5) is subject to negative resolution within the meaning of section 41(6) of the Interpretation Act (Northern Ireland) 1954 (c. 33 (N.I.)).

## 67 Interpretation

In this Act—

"the Board" means the Commissioners of Inland Revenue,

"modifications" includes alterations, additions and omissions, and "modifies" is to be construed accordingly,

"the Northern Ireland Department" means the Department for Social Development in Northern Ireland,

"prescribed" means prescribed by regulations, and

"tax credit" and "tax credits" have the meanings given by section 1(2).

## 68 Financial provision

(1) There is to be paid out of money provided by Parliament—

(a) any expenditure of a Minister of the Crown or government department under this Act, and

(b) any increase attributable to this Act in sums payable out of money provided by Parliament under any other Act.

(2) There is to be paid into the Consolidated Fund any sums received by a government department by virtue of this Act (apart from any required by any other enactment to be paid into the National Insurance Fund).

## 69 Extent

(1) The amendments, repeals and revocations made by this Act have the same extent as the enactments or instruments to which they relate.

(2) Subject to that, this Act extends to Northern Ireland (as well as to England and Wales and Scotland).

## 70 Short title

This Act may be cited as the Tax Credits Act 2002.

# SCHEDULES

## SCHEDULE 1

Section 27

RIGHTS OF EMPLOYEES

*Right not to suffer detriment: Great Britain*

1 (1) The Employment Rights Act 1996 (c. 18) has effect subject to the following amendments.

(2) After section 47C insert—

**"47D Tax credits**

**"47D Tax credits**

(1) An employee has the right not to be subjected to any detriment by any act, or any deliberate failure to act, by his employer, done on the ground that—

(a) any action was taken, or was proposed to be taken, by or on behalf of the employee with a view to enforcing, or otherwise securing the benefit of, a right conferred on the employee by regulations under section 25 of the Tax Credits Act 2002,

(b) a penalty was imposed on the employer, or proceedings for a penalty were brought against him, under that Act, as a result of action taken by or on behalf of the employee for the purpose of enforcing, or otherwise securing the benefit of, such a right, or

(c) the employee is entitled, or will or may be entitled, to working tax credit.

(2) It is immaterial for the purposes of subsection (1)(a) or (b)—

(a) whether or not the employee has the right, or

(b) whether or not the right has been infringed,

but, for those provisions to apply, the claim to the right and (if applicable) the claim that it has been infringed must be made in good faith.

(3) Subsections (1) and (2) apply to a person who is not an employee within the meaning of this Act but who is an employee within the meaning of section 25 of the Tax Credits Act 2002, with references to his employer in those subsections (and sections 48(2) and (4) and 49(1)) being construed in accordance with that section.

(4) Subsections (1) and (2) do not apply to an employee if the detriment in question amounts to dismissal (within the meaning of Part 10)."

(3) In section 48 (complaints to employment tribunals), after subsection (1A) insert—

"(1B) A person may present a complaint to an employment tribunal that he has been subjected to a detriment in contravention of section 47D."

(4) In section 49 (remedies), at the end insert—

"(7) Where—

(a) the complaint is made under section 48(1B) by a person who is not an employee, and

(b) the detriment to which he is subjected is the termination of his contract with the person who is his employer for the purposes of section 25 of the Tax Credits Act 2002,

any compensation must not exceed the compensation that would be payable under Chapter 2 of Part 10 if the complainant had been an employee and had been dismissed for the reason specified in section 104B."

(5) In section 192(2)(aa) (armed forces)—

(a) for "section 45A," substitute "sections 45A, 47C and 47D,", and

(b) for "that section" substitute "those sections".

(6) In—

(a) section 194(2)(c) (House of Lords staff), and

(b) section 195(2)(c) (House of Commons staff),

for "and 47C" substitute ", 47C and 47D".

*Right not to suffer detriment: Northern Ireland*

2 (1) The Employment Rights (Northern Ireland) Order 1996 (S.I. 1996/1919 (N.I. 16)) has effect subject to the following amendments.

(2) After Article 70C insert—

**Tax credits**

"70D **Tax credits**

(1) An employee has the right not to be subjected to any detriment by any act, or any deliberate failure to act, by his employer, done on the ground that—

(a) any action was taken, or was proposed to be taken, by or on behalf of the employee with a view to enforcing, or otherwise securing the benefit of, a right conferred on the employee by regulations under section 25 of the Tax Credits Act 2002,

(b) a penalty was imposed on the employer, or proceedings for a penalty were brought against him, under that Act, as a result of action taken by or on behalf of the employee for the purpose of enforcing, or otherwise securing the benefit of, such a right, or

(c) the employee is entitled, or will or may be entitled, to working tax credit.

(2) It is immaterial for the purposes of paragraph (1)(a) or (b)—

(a) whether or not the employee has the right, or

(b) whether or not the right has been infringed,

but, for those provisions to apply, the claim to the right and (if applicable) the claim that it has been infringed must be made in good faith.

(3) Paragraphs (1) and (2) apply to a person who is not an employee within the meaning of this Order but who is an employee within the meaning of section 25 of the Tax Credits Act 2002, with references to his employer in those paragraphs (and Articles 71(2) and (4) and 72(1)) being construed in accordance with that section.

(4) Paragraphs (1) and (2) do not apply to an employee if the detriment in question amounts to dismissal (within the meaning of Part 11)."

(3) In Article 71 (complaints to industrial tribunals), after paragraph (1A) insert—

"(1B) A person may present a complaint to an industrial tribunal that he has been subjected to a detriment in contravention of Article 70D."

(4) In Article 72 (remedies), at the end insert—

"(7) Where—

(a) the complaint is made under Article 71(1B) by a person who is not an employee, and

(b) the detriment to which he is subjected is the termination of his contract with the person who is his employer for the purposes of section 25 of the Tax Credits Act 2002,

any compensation must not exceed the compensation that would be payable under Chapter 2 of Part 11 if the complainant had been an employee and had been dismissed for the reason specified in Article 135B."

(5) In Article 237(2)(aa) (armed forces)—

(a) for "Article 68A" substitute "Articles 68A, 70C and 70D", and

(b) for "that Article" substitute "those Articles".

*Right not to be unfairly dismissed: Great Britain*

3 (1) The Employment Rights Act 1996 (c. 18) has effect subject to the following amendments.

(2) For section 104B substitute—

**"104B Tax credits**

**"104B Tax credits**

(1) An employee who is dismissed shall be regarded for the purposes of this Part as unfairly dismissed if the reason (or, if more than one, the principal reason) for the dismissal is that—

(a) any action was taken, or was proposed to be taken, by or on behalf of the employee with a view to enforcing, or otherwise securing the benefit of, a right conferred on the employee by regulations under section 25 of the Tax Credits Act 2002,

(b) a penalty was imposed on the employer, or proceedings for a penalty were brought against him, under that Act, as a result of action taken by or on behalf of the employee for the purpose of enforcing, or otherwise securing the benefit of, such a right, or

(c) the employee is entitled, or will or may be entitled, to working tax credit.

(2) It is immaterial for the purposes of subsection (1)(a) or (b)—

(a) whether or not the employee has the right, or

(b) whether or not the right has been infringed,

but, for those provisions to apply, the claim to the right and (if applicable) the claim that it has been infringed must be made in good faith."

(3) In section 105 (redundancy as unfair dismissal), after subsection (7A) continue to insert—

"(7B) This subsection applies if the reason (or, if more than one, the principal reason) for which the employee was selected for dismissal was one of those specified in subsection (1) of section 104B (read with subsection (2) of that section)."

(4) In section 108(3) (cases where no qualifying period of employment is required) and section 109(2) (cases where upper age limit does not apply), after paragraph (gg) continue to insert—

"(gh) subsection (1) of section 104B (read with subsection (2) of that section) applies,".

*Right not to be unfairly dismissed: Northern Ireland*

4 (1) The Employment Rights (Northern Ireland) Order 1996 (S.I. 1996/1919 (N.I. 16)) has effect subject to the following amendments.

(2) For Article 135B substitute—

**Tax credits**

"135B **Tax credits**

(1) An employee who is dismissed shall be regarded for the purposes of this Part as unfairly dismissed if the reason (or, if more than one, the principal reason) for the dismissal is that—

(a) any action was taken, or was proposed to be taken, by or on behalf of the employee with a view to enforcing, or otherwise securing the benefit of, a right conferred on the employee by regulations under section 25 of the Tax Credits Act 2002,

(b) a penalty was imposed on the employer, or proceedings for a penalty were brought against him, under that Act, as a result of action taken by or on behalf of the employee for the purpose of enforcing, or otherwise securing the benefit of, such a right, or

(c) the employee is entitled, or will or may be entitled, to working tax credit.

(2) It is immaterial for the purposes of paragraph (1)(a) or (b)—

(a) whether or not the employee has the right, or

(b) whether or not the right has been infringed,

but, for those provisions to apply, the claim to the right and (if applicable) the claim that it has been infringed must be made in good faith."

(3) In Article 137 (redundancy as unfair dismissal), after paragraph (6A) continue to insert—

"(6B) This paragraph applies if the reason (or, if more than one, the principal reason) for which the employee was selected for dismissal was one of those specified in paragraph (1) of Article 135B (read with paragraph (2) of that Article)."

(4) In Article 140(3) (cases where no qualifying period of employment is required) and Article 141(2) (cases where upper age limit does not apply), after sub-paragraph (ff) continue to insert—

"(fg) paragraph (1) of Article 135B (read with paragraph (2) of that Article) applies,".

## SCHEDULE 2

Section 34

### PENALTIES: SUPPLEMENTARY

*Determination of penalties by Board*

1 (1) The Board may make a determination—

(a) imposing a penalty under section 31, 32(2)(b) or (3) or 33, and

(b) setting it at such amount as, in their opinion, is appropriate.

(2) The Board must give notice of a determination of a penalty under this paragraph to the person on whom the penalty is imposed.

(3) The notice must state the date on which it is given and give details of the right to appeal against the determination under section 38.

(4) After the notice of a determination under this paragraph has been given the determination must not be altered except on appeal.

(5) A penalty determined under this paragraph becomes payable at the end of the period of thirty days beginning with the date on which the notice of determination is given.

2 (1) On an appeal to them under section 38 against the determination of a penalty under paragraph 1, the General Commissioners or Special Commissioners may—

(a) if it appears that no penalty has been incurred, set the determination aside,

(b) if the amount determined appears to be appropriate, confirm the determination,

(c) if the amount determined appears to be excessive, reduce it to such other amount (including nil) as they consider appropriate, or

(d) if the amount determined appears to be insufficient, increase it to such amount not exceeding the permitted maximum as they consider appropriate.

(2) An appeal from a decision of the Commissioners under sub-paragraph (1) lies, at the instance of the person on whom the penalty was imposed, to—

(a) the High Court, or

(b) in Scotland, the Court of Session as the Court of Exchequer in Scotland,

and on such an appeal the court has a similar jurisdiction to that conferred on the Commissioners by sub-paragraph (1).

*Penalty proceedings before Commissioners*

3 (1) The Board may commence proceedings for a penalty under section 32(2)(a).

(2) Proceedings under this paragraph are by way of information in writing, made to the General Commissioners or Special Commissioners, and upon summons issued by them to the defendant (or defender) to appear before them at a time and place stated in the summons; and they must hear and decide each case in a summary way.

4 (1) An appeal against the determination of a penalty in proceedings under paragraph 3 lies to the High Court or, in Scotland, the Court of Session as the Court of Exchequer in Scotland—

(a) by any party on a question of law, and

(b) by the defendant (or, in Scotland, the defender) against the amount of the penalty.

(2) On any such appeal the court may—

(a) if it appears that no penalty has been incurred, set the determination aside,

(b) if the amount determined appears to be appropriate, confirm the determination,

(c) if the amount determined appears to be excessive, reduce it to such other amount (including nil) as the court considers appropriate, or

(d) if the amount determined appears to be insufficient, increase it to such amount not exceeding the permitted maximum as the court considers appropriate.

*Mitigation of penalties*

5 The Board may in their discretion mitigate any penalty under this Part or stay or compound any proceedings for any such penalty and may also, after judgment, further mitigate or entirely remit any such penalty.

*Time limits for penalties*

6 (1) In the case of a penalty under section 31 relating to a tax credit for a person or persons for the whole or part of a tax year (other than a penalty to which sub-paragraph (3) applies), the Board may determine the penalty at any time before the latest of—

(a) the end of the period of one year beginning with the expiry of the period for initiating an enquiry under section 19 into the entitlement of the person, or the joint entitlement of the persons, for the tax year,

(b) if such an enquiry is made, the end of the period of one year beginning with the day on which the enquiry is completed, and

(c) if a decision relating to the entitlement of the person, or the joint entitlement of the persons, for the tax year is made under section 20(1) or (4), the end of the period of one year beginning with the day on which the decision is made.

(2) In the case of a penalty under section 32 relating to a tax credit for a person or persons for the whole or part of a tax year (other than a penalty to which sub-paragraph (3) applies), the Board may determine the penalty, or commence proceedings for it, at any time before—

(a) if an enquiry into the entitlement of the person, or the joint entitlement of the persons, for the tax year is made under section 19, the end of the period of one year beginning with the day on which the enquiry is completed, and

(b) otherwise, the end of the period of one year beginning with the expiry of the period for initiating such an enquiry.

(3) In the case of—

(a) a penalty under section 31 or 32 relating to a requirement imposed by virtue of regulations under section 25, or

(b) a penalty under section 33,

the Board may determine the penalty, or commence proceedings for it, at any time before the end of the period of six years after the date on which the penalty was incurred or began to be incurred.

*Recovery of penalties*

7 (1) A penalty payable under this Part is to be treated for the purposes of Part 6 of the Taxes Management Act 1970 (c. 9) (collection and recovery) as if it were tax charged in an assessment and due and payable.

(2) Regulations under section 203(2)(a) of the Income and Corporation Taxes Act 1988 (c. 1) (PAYE) apply to a penalty payable under this Part as if it were an underpayment of tax for a previous year of assessment.

## SCHEDULE 3

Section 47

### TAX CREDITS: CONSEQUENTIAL AMENDMENTS

*Attachment of Earnings Act 1971 (c. 32)*

1 In section 24 of the Attachment of Earnings Act 1971 (meaning of "earnings" for the purposes of attachment of earnings orders), in subsection (2) (sums which are not earnings), after paragraph (b) insert—

"(ba) a tax credit (within the meaning of the Tax Credits Act 2002);".

*Magistrates' Courts Act 1980 (c. 43)*

2 In Part 1 of Schedule 6 to the Magistrates' Court Act 1980 (fees to be taken by justices' chief executives), in paragraph 1(a) of the Note at the end—

(a) for "or working families' tax credit under sections 124 and 128 of the Social Security Contributions and Benefits Act 1992 (c. 4) or" substitute "under section 124 of the Social Security Contributions and Benefits Act 1992,", and

(b) after "2002)" insert ", of any element of child tax credit other than the family element or of working tax credit".

*Judgments Enforcement (Northern Ireland) Order 1981 (S.I. 1981/226 (N.I. 6))*

3 In Article 3 of the Judgments Enforcement (Northern Ireland) Order 1981 (meaning of "earnings" for the purposes of attachment of earnings orders), in paragraph (5) (sums which are not earnings), after sub-paragraph (b) insert—

"(ba) a tax credit (within the meaning of the Tax Credits Act 2002);".

*Legal Aid, Advice and Assistance (Northern Ireland) Order 1981 (S.I. 1981/228 (N.I. 8))*

4 The Legal Aid, Advice and Assistance (Northern Ireland) Order 1981 has effect subject to the following amendments.

5 In Article 3(1)(b) (persons eligible for advice and assistance), for the words after "income support" substitute "or an income-based jobseeker's allowance (payable under the Jobseekers (Northern Ireland) Order 1995 (S.I. 1995/2705 (N.I. 15)))".

6 In Article 7(2) (contributions from persons receiving advice or assistance), for the words from ", an income-based" to "family credit" substitute "or an income-based jobseeker's allowance (payable under the Jobseekers (Northern Ireland) Order 1995)".

7 In Article 14(5) (assessment of disposable capital and income and of maximum contribution), for the words after "income support" substitute "or an income-based jobseeker's allowance (payable under the Jobseekers (Northern Ireland) Order 1995)".

*Magistrates' Courts (Northern Ireland) Order 1981 (S.I. 1981/1675 (N.I. 26))*

8 In Article 100 of the Magistrates' Courts (Northern Ireland) Order 1981 (meaning of "earnings" for the purposes of attachment of earnings orders), in paragraph (5) (sums which are not earnings), after sub-paragraph (b) insert—

"(ba) a tax credit (within the meaning of the Tax Credits Act 2002);".

*Transport Act 1982 (c. 49)*

9 In section 70(2)(b) of the Transport Act 1982 (applicants for exemption from wearing of seat belts in the case of whom the Secretary of State may make payments in respect of medical examinations), for ", working families' tax credit or disabled person's tax credit" substitute ", any element of child tax credit other than the family element or working tax credit".

*Legal Aid (Scotland) Act 1986 (c. 47)*

10 The Legal Aid (Scotland) Act 1986 has effect subject to the following amendments.

11 In section 8(b) (availability of advice and assistance to persons in receipt of certain benefits), for the words after "receipt of" substitute "income support or an income-based jobseeker's allowance (payable under the Jobseekers Act 1995 (c. 18)),".

12 In section 11(2)(b) (no clients' contributions by persons in receipt of certain benefits), for the words after "receipt of" substitute "income support or an income-based jobseeker's allowance (payable under the Jobseekers Act 1995),".

*Debtors (Scotland) Act 1987 (c. 18)*

13 In section 73(3) of the Debtors (Scotland) Act 1987 (sums which are not earnings), after paragraph (d) insert—

"(da) a tax credit (within the meaning of the Tax Credits Act 2002);".

*Income and Corporation Taxes Act 1988 (c. 1)*

14 In the Income and Corporation Taxes Act 1988, after section 617 insert—

*"617A Tax credits under Part 1 of Tax Credits Act 2002*

617A Payments of a tax credit, within the meaning of the Tax Credits Act 2002, shall not be treated as income for any purpose of the Income Tax Acts."

*Children Act 1989 (c. 41)*

15 The Children Act 1989 has effect subject to the following amendments.

16 (1) Section 17 (provision of services for children in need) is amended as follows.

(2) In subsection (9)—

(a) for ", working families' tax credit or disabled person's tax credit under the" substitute "under", and

(b) after "1992" insert ", of any element of child tax credit other than the family element, of working tax credit".

(3) After subsection (11) insert—

"(12) The Treasury may by regulations prescribe circumstances in which a person is to be treated for the purposes of this Part (or for such of those purposes as are prescribed) as in receipt of any element of child tax credit other than the family element or of working tax credit."

17 In section 17A(5)(b) (direct payments: persons entitled to gross payments), before "or of" insert ", of any element of child tax credit other than the family element, of working tax credit".

18 In section 29(3) (no payment of charge for provision of services by local authority by persons in receipt of certain benefits)—

(a) for ", working families' tax credit or disabled person's tax credit under the" substitute "under", and

(b) after "1992" insert ", of any element of child tax credit other than the family element, of working tax credit".

19 In section 104 (regulations and orders), after "Lord Chancellor" insert ", the Treasury".

20 In paragraph 21(4) of Schedule 2 (no contribution towards maintenance by local authority by persons in receipt of certain benefits)—

(a) for ", working families' tax credit or disabled person's tax credit under the" substitute "under", and

(b) after "1992" insert ", of any element of child tax credit other than the family element, of working tax credit".

*Education Reform (Northern Ireland) Order 1989 (S.I. 1989/2406 (N.I. 20))*

21 In Article 131(3)(b) of the Education Reform (Northern Ireland) Order 1989 (remission of charges for board and lodging on a residential trip for parents in receipt of certain benefits), for ", working families' tax credit" substitute ", any element of child tax credit other than the family element, working tax credit".

*Child Support Act 1991 (c. 48)*

22 In section 47(3)(b) of the Child Support Act 1991 (no fees payable by persons in receipt of certain benefits), for "working families' tax credit" substitute "any element of child tax credit other than the family element, working tax credit".

*Child Support (Northern Ireland) Order 1991 (S.I. 1991/2628 (N.I. 23))*

23 In Article 44(2)(b) of the Child Support (Northern Ireland) Order 1991 (no fees payable by persons in receipt of certain benefits), for "working families' tax credit" substitute "any element of child tax credit other than the family element, working tax credit".

*Social Security Contributions and Benefits Act 1992 (c. 4)*

24 The Social Security Contributions and Benefits Act 1992 has effect subject to the following amendments.

25 In section 30C (incapacity benefit), for subsection (5) substitute—

"(5) Where a person claims the higher rate of short-term incapacity benefit, or long-term incapacity benefit, under section 30A above for a period commencing after he has ceased to be in qualifying remunerative work (within the meaning of Part 1 of the Tax Credits Act 2002) and—

(a) the day following that on which he so ceased was a day of incapacity for work for him,

(b) he has been entitled to the higher rate of short-term incapacity benefit, or to long-term incapacity benefit, under section 30A above within the period of two years ending with that day of incapacity for work, and

(c) he satisfied the relevant tax credit conditions on the day before he so ceased,

every day during that period on which he satisfied those conditions is to be treated for the purposes of the claim as a day of incapacity for work for him.

(5A) A person satisfies the relevant tax credit conditions on a day if—

(a) he is entitled for the day to the disability element of working tax credit (on a claim made by him or by him jointly with another) or would be so entitled but for the fact that the relevant income (within the meaning of Part 1 of the Tax Credits Act 2002) in his or their case is such that he is not so entitled, and

(b) either working tax credit or any element of child tax credit other than the family element is paid in respect of the day on such a claim."

26 In section 37(2) (widowed mother's allowance), for "81(2)" substitute "77(5)".

27 In section 39(1), (2) and (3) (rate of widowed mother's allowance and widow's pension), for "sections 44 and" continue to substitute "sections 44 to".

28 In section 39A(3) (widowed parent's allowance), for "81(2)" substitute "77(5)".

29 In section 39C(1), (3) and (4) (rate of widowed parent's allowance and bereavement allowance), for "45A" substitute "45".

30 In section 42 (long-term incapacity benefit for widows and widowers), for subsection (1) substitute—

"(1) Where a person claims incapacity benefit under section 40 or 41 above for a period commencing after he has ceased to be in qualifying remunerative work (within the meaning of Part 1 of the Tax Credits Act 2002) and—

(a) the day following that on which he so ceased was a day of incapacity for work for him,

(b) he has been entitled to incapacity benefit under that section within the period of two years ending with that day of incapacity for work, and

(c) he satisfied the relevant tax credit conditions on the day before he so ceased,

every day during that period on which he satisfied those conditions is to be treated for the purposes of the claim as a day of incapacity for work for him.

(1A) A person satisfies the relevant tax credit conditions on a day if—

(a) he is entitled for the day to the disability element of working tax credit (on a claim made by him or by him jointly with another) or would be so entitled but for the fact that the relevant income (within the meaning of Part 1 of the Tax Credits Act 2002) in his or their case is such that he is not so entitled, and

(b) either working tax credit or any element of child tax credit other than the family element is paid in respect of the day on such a claim."

31 In section 48BB(5) and (6) (entitlement to category B retirement pension by reference to certain benefits), for "45A" substitute "45".

32 In section 51(2) and (3) (category B retirement pension for widowers), for "45A" substitute "45".

33 In section 60(4) and (5) (failure to satisfy contribution conditions), for "subsections (6) and (7)" substitute "subsection (7)".

34 In section 114(4) (cost of providing for children), for "81" substitute "82".

*Social Security Administration Act 1992 (c. 5)*

35 In section 150(1)(h) of the Social Security Administration Act 1992 (up-rating of benefits), after "section 135(1)" insert "of that Act".

*Social Security Contributions and Benefits (Northern Ireland) Act 1992 (c. 7)*

36 The Social Security Contributions and Benefits (Northern Ireland) Act 1992 has effect subject to the following amendments.

37 In section 30C (incapacity benefit), for subsection (5) substitute—

"(5) Where a person claims the higher rate of short-term incapacity benefit, or long-term incapacity benefit, under section 30A above for a period commencing after he has ceased to be in qualifying remunerative work (within the meaning of Part 1 of the Tax Credits Act 2002) and—

(a) the day following that on which he so ceased was a day of incapacity for work for him,

(b) he has been entitled to the higher rate of short-term incapacity benefit, or to long-term incapacity benefit, under section 30A above within the period of two years ending with that day of incapacity for work, and

(c) he satisfied the relevant tax credit conditions on the day before he so ceased,

every day during that period on which he satisfied those conditions is to be treated for the purposes of the claim as a day of incapacity for work for him.

(5A) A person satisfies the relevant tax credit conditions on a day if—

(a) he is entitled for the day to the disability element of working tax credit (on a claim made by him or by him jointly with another) or would be so entitled but for the fact that the relevant income (within the meaning of Part 1 of the Tax Credits Act 2002) in his or their case is such that he is not so entitled, and

(b) either working tax credit or any element of child tax credit other than the family element is paid in respect of the day on such a claim."

38 In section 37(2) (widowed mother's allowance), for "81(2)" substitute "77(5)".

39 In section 39(1), (2) and (3) (rate of widowed mother's allowance and widow's pension), for "sections 44 and" continue to substitute "sections 44 to".

40 In section 39A(3) (widowed parent's allowance), for "81(2)" substitute "77(5)".

41 In section 39C(1), (3) and (4) (rate of widowed parent's allowance and bereavement allowance), for "45A" substitute "45".

42 In section 42 (long-term incapacity benefit for widows and widowers), for subsection (1) substitute—

"(1) Where a person claims incapacity benefit under section 40 or 41 above for a period commencing after he has ceased to be in qualifying remunerative work (within the meaning of Part 1 of the Tax Credits Act 2002) and—

(a) the day following that on which he so ceased was a day of incapacity for work for him,

(b) he has been entitled to incapacity benefit under that section within the period of two years ending with that day of incapacity for work, and

(c) he satisfied the relevant tax credit conditions on the day before he so ceased,

every day during that period on which he satisfied those conditions is to be treated for the purposes of the claim as a day of incapacity for work for him.

(1A) A person satisfies the relevant tax credit conditions on a day if—

(a) he is entitled for the day to the disability element of working tax credit (on a claim made by him or by him jointly with another) or would be so entitled but for the fact that the relevant income (within the meaning of Part 1 of the Tax Credits Act 2002) in his or their case is such that he is not so entitled, and

(b) either working tax credit or any element of child tax credit other than the family element is paid in respect of the day on such a claim."

43 In section 48BB(5) and (6) (entitlement to category B retirement pension by reference to certain benefits), for "45A" substitute "45".

44 In section 51(2) and (3) (category B retirement pension for widowers), for "45A" substitute "45".

45 In section 60(4) and (5) (failure to satisfy contribution conditions), for "subsections (6) and (7)" substitute "subsection (7)".

46 In section 114(4) (cost of providing for children), for "81" substitute "82".

*Value Added Tax Act 1994 (c. 23)*

47 The Value Added Tax Act 1994 has effect subject to the following amendments.

48 In Schedule 7A, in paragraph 6(2)(c) in Group 3 (reduced rate on grant-funded installation of heating equipment, security goods and connection of gas supply: persons in receipt of certain benefits), for "disabled person's tax credit, working families' tax credit," substitute "any element of child tax credit other than the family element, working tax credit,".

49 In Schedule 8, in Note (1D) in Group 15 (zero-rating: charities), for paragraphs (e) and (f) substitute—

"(e) any element of child tax credit other than the family element; and

(f) working tax credit."

*Children (Scotland) Act 1995 (c. 36)*

50 In section 22(4) of the Children (Scotland) Act 1995 (no repayment of assistance given by local authority by persons in receipt of certain benefits), after "1992;" insert—

"(aa) any element of child tax credit other than the family element or working tax credit;".

*Children (Northern Ireland) Order 1995 (S.I. 1995/755 (N.I. 2))*

51 The Children (Northern Ireland) Order 1995 has effect subject to the following amendments.

52 (1) Article 18 (duty of authority to provide personal social services for children in need) is amended as follows.

(2) In paragraph (9), for "working families' tax credit or disabled person's tax credit" substitute "of any element of child tax credit other than the family element, of working tax credit".

(3) After that paragraph insert—

"(10) The Treasury may by regulations prescribe circumstances in which a person is to be treated for the purposes of this Part (or for such of those purposes as are prescribed) as in receipt of any element of child tax credit other than the family element or of working tax credit."

53 In Article 18C(7)(b) (direct payments), before "or of" insert ", of any element of child tax credit other than the family element, of working tax credit".

54 In Article 24(3) (no payment of charge for provision of services by Health and Social Services Board by persons in receipt of certain benefits), for "working families' tax credit or disabled person's tax credit" substitute "of any element of child tax credit other than the family element, of working tax credit".

55 In Article 39(4) (no contribution towards maintenance by Health and Social Services Board by persons in receipt of certain benefits), for "working families' tax credit or disabled person's tax credit" substitute "of any element of child tax credit other than the family element, of working tax credit".

56 (1) Article 183 (regulations and orders) is amended as follows.

(2) In paragraph (1), for "and (3)" insert "to (4)".

(3) After paragraph (3) insert—

> "(4) Regulations under Article 18(10) shall be made by statutory instrument which shall be subject to annulment in pursuance of a resolution of either House of Parliament."

*Road Traffic (Northern Ireland) Order 1995 (S.I. 1995/2994 (N.I. 18))*

57 In Article 25(2)(b) of the Road Traffic (Northern Ireland) Order 1995 (applicants for exemption from wearing of seat belts in the case of whom the Department of the Environment in Northern Ireland may make payments in respect of medical examinations), for "working families' tax credit or disabled person's tax credit" substitute "any element of child tax credit other than the family element or working tax credit".

*Housing Grants, Construction and Regeneration Act 1996 (c. 53)*

58 In section 77(1)(e) of the Housing Grants, Construction and Regeneration Act 1996 (entitlement to home repair assistance), for "working families' tax credit, housing benefit, council tax benefit or disabled person's tax credit" substitute "housing benefit, council tax benefit, any element of child tax credit other than the family element or working tax credit".

*Finance Act 2000 (c. 17)*

59 In paragraph 17(1) of Schedule 20 to the Finance Act 2000 (tax relief for research and development: amount of PAYE and NICs liabilities)—

(a) in paragraph (a), for "the working families' tax credit or disabled person's tax credit", and

(b) in paragraph (b), for "working families' tax credit or disabled person's tax credit",

substitute "child tax credit or working tax credit".

## SCHEDULE 4

Section 51

TRANSFER OF FUNCTIONS: CONSEQUENTIAL AMENDMENTS

*Social Security Administration Act 1992 (c. 5)*

1 The Social Security Administration Act 1992 has effect subject to the following amendments.

2 In section 71(8) (recovery of benefits by deduction from prescribed benefits), after "amount paid" insert ", other than an amount paid in respect of child benefit or guardian's allowance,".

3 In section 189(8) (powers to make orders exercisable only with Treasury consent), after "made" insert "by the Secretary of State".

*Social Security Contributions and Benefits (Northern Ireland) Act 1992 (c. 7)*

4 The Social Security Contributions and Benefits (Northern Ireland) Act 1992 has effect subject to the following amendments.

5 In section 171(1) (regulations and orders to be made by the Northern Ireland Department except where provision of the Act otherwise provides), after "to" insert "any provision providing for regulations or orders to be made by the Treasury or the Commissioners of Inland Revenue and to".

6 In section 172(11A) (regulations subject to draft affirmative Parliamentary procedure), for "or 118" substitute ", 118 or 141".

*Social Security Administration (Northern Ireland) Act 1992 (c. 8)*

7 The Social Security Administration (Northern Ireland) Act 1992 has effect subject to the following amendments.

8 In section 69(8) (recovery of benefits by deduction from prescribed benefits), after "amount paid" insert ", other than an amount paid in respect of child benefit or guardian's allowance,".

9 In sections 132(1) and 133 (orders for uprating of benefits corresponding to those made for Great Britain by Secretary of State), after "Secretary of State" insert "or the Treasury".

10 In section 165(3) (powers to make regulations and orders which are exercisable by statutory rule), after "Act" insert "on the Department or the Lord Chancellor".

11 (1) Section 166 (Parliamentary and Assembly control of orders and regulations) is amended as follows.

(2) In subsection (5), for the words from "in like" to the end substitute "(in the case of regulations made by the Lord Chancellor in like manner as a statutory instrument, with section 5 of the Statutory Instruments Act 1946 (c. 36) applying accordingly)".

(3) In subsection (10A), after "129" insert ", 132, 133, 134".

*Social Security Act 1998 (c. 14)*

12 The Social Security Act 1998 has effect subject to the following amendments.

13 (1) Section 79 (regulations and orders) is amended as follows.

(2) In subsection (1), for "subsection (2)" substitute "subsections (2) and (2A)".

(3) After subsection (2) insert—

"(2A) Subsection (1) has effect subject to any provision providing for regulations to be made by the Treasury or the Commissioners of Inland Revenue."

14 In section 80(2) (negative Parliamentary procedure for regulations made by Secretary of State), after "Secretary of State" insert ", the Treasury or the Commissioners of Inland Revenue".

15 References in Chapter 2 of Part 1 (social security decisions and appeals) to a decision of the Secretary of State are, where the context so requires in consequence of section 50, to be construed as references to a decision of the Board (or, where the power to decide is exercised by an officer of the Board, an officer of the Board).

*Social Security (Northern Ireland) Order 1998 (S.I. 1998/1506 (N.I. 10))*

16 The Social Security (Northern Ireland) Order 1998 has effect subject to the following amendments.

17 (1) Article 74 (regulations and orders) is amended as follows.

(2) In paragraph (1), for "paragraph (2)" substitute "paragraphs (2) and (2A)".

(3) After paragraph (2) insert—

"(2A) Paragraph (1) has effect subject to any provision providing for regulations to be made by the Treasury or the Commissioners of Inland Revenue.

(2B) Powers of the Treasury or the Commissioners of Inland Revenue to make regulations under this Order are exercisable by statutory instrument."

18 (1) Article 75 (Assembly etc. control of regulations) is amended as follows.

(2) In paragraph (1), for "The regulations to which this paragraph applies" substitute "Where regulations specified in paragraph (2) are made by the Department, they".

(3) After that paragraph insert—

"(1A) Where regulations specified in paragraph (2) fall to be made by the Treasury or the Commissioners of Inland Revenue they shall not be made unless a draft of the instrument containing them has been laid before Parliament and approved by a resolution of each House of Parliament."

(4) In paragraph (2), for "Paragraph (1) applies to" substitute "The regulations specified in this paragraph are".

(5) In paragraph (3), for "to which paragraph (1) applies" substitute "specified in paragraph (2)".

(6) After that paragraph insert—

"(3A) Regulations made under this Order by the Treasury or the Commissioners of Inland Revenue, other than regulations specified in paragraph (2), shall be subject to annulment in pursuance of a resolution of either House of Parliament."

19 References in Chapter 2 of Part 2 (social security decisions and appeals) to a decision of the Department are, where the context so requires in consequence of section 50, to be construed as references to a decision of the Board (or, where the power to decide is exercised by an officer of the Board, an officer of the Board).

*Immigration and Asylum Act 1999 (c. 33)*

20 The Immigration and Asylum Act 1999 has effect subject to the following amendments.

21 In section 115(5) and (6) (exclusion of persons subject to immigration control from certain benefits), for "the benefits mentioned in subsection (1)(f) or (g)" substitute "child benefit".

22 (1) Section 123(9) (regulations about back-dating of benefits where person recorded as refugee) is amended as follows.

(2) After paragraph (b) insert—

"(ba) in relation to child benefit (and guardian's allowance), regulations made by the Treasury;".

(3) In paragraphs (c) and (d), after "benefit" insert "(apart from child benefit and guardian's allowance)".

## SCHEDULE 5

Section 59

### USE AND DISCLOSURE OF INFORMATION

*Powers to use information*

1 Information which is held for the purposes of any functions relating to tax credits, child benefit or guardian's allowance—

(a) by the Board, or

(b) by a person providing services to the Board, in connection with the provision of those services,

may be used, or supplied to any person providing services to the Board, for the purposes of, or for any purposes connected with, the exercise of any such functions.

2 (1) Information which is held for the purposes of any functions relating to tax credits, child benefit or guardian's allowance—

(a) by the Board, or

(b) by a person providing services to the Board, in connection with the provision of those services,

may be used, or supplied to any person providing services to the Board, for the purposes of, or for any purposes connected with, the exercise of any other functions of the Board.

(2) Information which is held for the purposes of any functions other than those relating to tax credits, child benefit or guardian's allowance—

(a) by the Board, or

(b) by a person providing services to the Board, in connection with the provision of those services, may be used, or supplied to any person providing services to the Board, for the purposes of, or for any purposes connected with, the exercise of any functions of the Board relating to tax credits, child benefit or guardian's allowance.

3 (1) Information which is held for the purposes of any functions relating to social security (including child benefit and guardian's allowance) or tax credits—

(a) by the Secretary of State or the Northern Ireland Department, or

(b) by a person providing services to the Secretary of State or the Northern Ireland Department, in connection with the provision of those services,

may be used, or supplied to any person providing services to the Secretary of State or the Northern Ireland Department, for the purposes of, or for any purposes connected with, the exercise of any functions under relevant regulations.

(2) In this paragraph "relevant regulations" are regulations made under—

(a) section 4, 6 or 58 of this Act,

(b) section 5 of the Social Security Administration Act 1992 (c. 5), or

(c) section 5 of the Social Security Administration (Northern Ireland) Act 1992 (c. 8).

*Exchange of information between Board and Secretary of State or Northern Ireland Departments*

4 (1) This paragraph applies to information which is held for the purposes of functions relating to tax credits, child benefit or guardian's allowance—

(a) by the Board, or

(b) by a person providing services to the Board, in connection with the provision of those services.

(2) Information to which this paragraph applies may be supplied—

(a) to the Secretary of State or the Northern Ireland Department, or

(b) to a person providing services to the Secretary of State or the Northern Ireland Department,

for use for the purposes of functions relating to social security, child support or war pensions or for such purposes relating to evaluation or statistical studies as may be prescribed.

(3) An authorised officer may require information to which this paragraph applies to be supplied—

(a) to the Secretary of State or the Northern Ireland Department, or

(b) to a person providing services to the Secretary of State or the Northern Ireland Department,

for use for the purposes of functions relating to social security or child support.

(4) In sub-paragraph (3) "authorised officer" means an officer of the Secretary of State or the Northern Ireland Department authorised for the purposes of this paragraph by the Secretary of State or the Northern Ireland Department.

(5) In this paragraph "war pension" has the meaning given by section 25(4) of the Social Security Act 1989 (c. 24).

5 (1) This paragraph applies to information which is held for the purposes of functions relating to tax credits, child benefit or guardian's allowance—

(a) by the Board, or

(b) by a person providing services to the Board, in connection with the provision of those services.

(2) Information to which this paragraph applies may be supplied—

(a) to the Secretary of State or the Department for Employment and Learning in Northern Ireland, or

(b) to a person providing services to the Secretary of State or that Department,

for use for the purposes of such functions relating to employment or training as may be prescribed.

6 (1) This paragraph applies to information which is held for the purposes of functions relating to social security, child support, war pensions, employment or training—

(a) by the Secretary of State or the Northern Ireland Department or the Department for Employment and Learning in Northern Ireland, or

(b) by a person providing services to the Secretary of State or either of those Departments, in connection with the provision of those services.

(2) Information to which this paragraph applies may be supplied—

(a) to the Board, or

(b) to a person providing services to the Board,

for use for the purposes of functions relating to tax credits, child benefit or guardian's allowance.

(3) The Board may require information to which this paragraph applies to be so supplied if the information is held for the purposes of functions relating to social security or child support.

(4) In this paragraph "war pension" has the meaning given by section 25(4) of the Social Security Act 1989.

*Exchange of information between Board and authorities administering certain benefits*

7 (1) This paragraph applies to information which is held for the purposes of functions relating to tax credits, child benefit or guardian's allowance—

(a) by the Board, or

(b) by a person providing services to the Board, in connection with the provision of those services.

(2) Information to which this paragraph applies may be supplied by or under the authority of the Board—

(a) to an authority administering housing benefit or council tax benefit, or

(b) to a person authorised to exercise any function of such an authority relating to such a benefit,

for use in the administration of such a benefit.

(3) Information supplied under this paragraph is not to be supplied by the recipient to any other person or body unless it is supplied—

(a) to a person to whom the information could be supplied directly by or under the authority of the Board,

(b) for the purposes of any civil or criminal proceedings relating to the Social Security Contributions and Benefits Act 1992 (c. 4), the Social Security

Administration Act 1992 (c. 5) or the Jobseekers Act 1995 (c. 18) or to any provision of Northern Ireland legislation corresponding to any of them, or

(c) under paragraph 8 below.

8 (1) The Board may require—

(a) an authority administering housing benefit or council tax benefit, or

(b) a person authorised to exercise any function of such an authority relating to such a benefit,

to supply benefit administration information held by the authority or other person to, or to a person providing services to, the Board for use for any purpose relating to tax credits, child benefit or guardian's allowance.

(2) In sub-paragraph (1) "benefit administration information", in relation to an authority or other person, means any information which is relevant to the exercise of any function relating to housing benefit or council tax benefit by the authority or other person.

*Provision of information by Board for health purposes*

9 (1) This paragraph applies to information which is held for the purposes of functions relating to tax credits, child benefit or guardian's allowance—

(a) by the Board, or

(b) by a person providing services to the Board, in connection with the provision of those services.

(2) Information to which this paragraph applies may be supplied—

(a) to the Secretary of State, the National Assembly for Wales, the Scottish Ministers or the Department of Health, Social Services and Public Safety in Northern Ireland, or

(b) to persons providing services to, or exercising functions on behalf of, the Secretary of State, the National Assembly for Wales, the Scottish Ministers or that Department,

for use for the purposes of such functions relating to health as may be prescribed.

(3) Information supplied under this paragraph is not to be supplied by the recipient to any other person or body unless it is supplied—

(a) to a person to whom the information could be supplied directly by or under the authority of the Board, or

(b) for the purpose of civil or criminal proceedings,

and is not to be so supplied in those circumstances without the authority of the Board.

(4) A person commits an offence if he discloses information supplied to him under this paragraph unless the disclosure is made—

(a) in accordance with sub-paragraph (3),

(b) in accordance with an enactment or an order of a court,

(c) with consent given by or on behalf of the person to whom the information relates, or

(d) in such a way as to prevent the identification of the person to whom it relates.

(5) It is a defence for a person charged with an offence under sub-paragraph (4) to prove that he reasonably believed that his disclosure was lawful.

(6) A person guilty of an offence under sub-paragraph (4) is liable—

(a) on conviction on indictment, to imprisonment for a term not exceeding two years, to a fine or to both, or

(b) on summary conviction, to imprisonment for a term not exceeding six months, to a fine not exceeding the statutory maximum or to both.

*Provision of information by Board for education purposes*

10 (1) This paragraph applies to information which is held for the purposes of functions relating to child benefit or guardian's allowance—

(a) by the Board, or

(b) by a person providing services to the Board, in connection with the provision of those services.

(2) Information to which this paragraph applies may be supplied to any civil servant or other person for the purpose of such functions relating to the provision of services of the kind mentioned in section 114(1) of the Learning and Skills Act 2000 (c. 21) (provision of services to encourage, enable or assist participation by young persons in education or training) as may be prescribed.

(3) Information supplied under this paragraph is not to be supplied by the recipient to any other person or body unless it is supplied—

(a) to a person to whom the information could be supplied directly by or under the authority of the Board, or

(b) for the purpose of civil or criminal proceedings,

and is not to be so supplied in those circumstances without the authority of the Board.

(4) A person commits an offence if he discloses information supplied to him under this paragraph unless the disclosure is made—

(a) in accordance with sub-paragraph (3),

(b) in accordance with an enactment or an order of the court,

(c) with consent given by or on behalf of the person to whom the information relates, or

(d) in such a way as to prevent the identification of the person to whom it relates.

(5) It is a defence for a person charged with an offence under sub-paragraph (4) to prove that he reasonably believed that his disclosure was lawful.

(6) A person guilty of an offence under sub-paragraph (4) is liable—

(a) on conviction on indictment, to imprisonment for a term not exceeding two years, to a fine or to both, or

(b) on summary conviction, to imprisonment for a term not exceeding six months, to a fine not exceeding the statutory maximum or to both.

*Unauthorised disclosure of information*

11 (1) Section 182 of the Finance Act 1989 (c. 26) (disclosure of information) is amended as follows.

(2) In subsection (1)—

(a) after "tax functions" continue to insert ", tax credit functions", and

(b) for paragraph (aa) substitute—

"(aa) to a tax credit in respect of any identifiable person,".

(3) For subsection (2AA) substitute—

"(2ZA) In this section "tax credit functions" means the functions relating to tax credits—

(a) of the Board,

(b) of any person carrying out the administrative work of the General Commissioners or the Special Commissioners, and

(c) of any other person providing, or employed in the provision of, services to the Board or to any person mentioned in paragraph (b) above."

(4) In subsection (2A), after "contributions," insert "child benefit, guardian's allowance,".

(5) In subsection (4)—

(a) in paragraph (b), after "tax functions" continue to insert ", tax credit functions",

(b) in paragraph (c), after "tax functions" continue to insert ", tax credit functions",

(c) for sub-paragraph (ia) of that paragraph substitute—

"(ia) to a tax credit in respect of any identifiable person,", and

(d) in sub-paragraph (iii) of that paragraph, after "to" insert "child benefit, guardian's allowance,".

(6) In subsection (5)(b), for ", to working families tax credit or disabled person's tax credit" substitute "or to a tax credit".

(7) In subsection (10), after "1989," insert—

"""tax credit" means a tax credit under the Tax Credits Act 2002,".

*Consequential amendments*

12 In—

(a) section 122(1)(a) of the Social Security Administration Act 1992 (c. 5), and

(b) section 116(1)(a) of the Social Security Administration (Northern Ireland) Act 1992 (c. 8),

(supply of information held by tax authorities for fraud prevention and verification), for "or paragraph 2 of Schedule 5 to the Tax Credits Act 1999" substitute "or paragraph 4 of Schedule 5 to the Tax Credits Act 2002".

13 In section 110(5A) of the Finance Act 1997 (c. 16) (obtaining by Board and Commissioners of Customs and Excise of information from social security authorities), for "paragraph 3 of Schedule 5 to the Tax Credits Act 1999 (supply to Inland Revenue for purposes of tax credit of information so held)" substitute "paragraph 6 of Schedule 5 to the Tax Credits Act 2002 (supply to Inland Revenue for purposes of tax credit, child benefit or guardian's allowance of information so held)".

## SCHEDULE 6

Section 60

### REPEALS AND REVOCATIONS

| *Title and reference* | *Extent of repeal or revocation* |
|---|---|
| Taxes Management Act 1970 (c. 9) | In section 36(3A), the words "or under Schedule 13B to that Act (elections as to transfer of children's tax credit)". |
| | In section 37A, the words "or partner" and the words "or paragraph 4 of Schedule 13B to that Act". |
| | In section 43A(2A), the words "or under Schedule 13B to that Act (elections as to transfer of children's tax credit)". |
| | In section 58(3)(b), the words ", paragraph 6 of Schedule 13B to that Act". |
| Social Security Act 1986 (c. 50) | In Schedule 10, paragraph 61. |
| Income and Corporation Taxes Act 1988 (c. 1) | Section 257AA. |
| | Section 257A(7) to (9). |
| | In section 257C(1) and (3), the words ", 257AA(2) and (2A)". |
| | In section 617, in subsection (1), paragraph (b) and the word "and" before it and, in subsection (2)(a), the words ", working families tax credit, disabled person's tax credit". |
| | Schedule 13B. |
| Children Act 1989 (c. 41) | In section 17A(5)(b), the words ", working families' tax credit or disabled person's tax credit". |
| Education Reform (Northern Ireland) Order 1989 (S.I. 1989/2406 (N.I. 20)) | In Article 131(3)(b), the words "or disabled person's tax credit". |
| Disability Living Allowance and Disability Working Allowance Act 1991 (c. 21) | In Schedule 3, Part 2. |
| Child Support Act 1991 (c. 48) | In section 54, the definition of "working families' tax credit". |
| Disability Living Allowance and Disability Working Allowance (Northern Ireland) Order 1991 (S.I. 1991/1712 (N.I. 17)) | In Schedule 3, paragraph 9. |
| Child Support (Northern Ireland) Order 1991 (S.I. 1991/2628 (N.I. 23)) | In Article 2(2), the definition of "working families' tax credit". |
| Social Security Contributions and Benefits Act 1992 (c. 4) | In section 20(1), the words "(with increase for child dependants)" (in each place) and, in paragraph (f)(i), the words "and child". |

| *Title and reference* | *Extent of repeal or revocation* |
|---|---|
| | In section 21(5A)(b), the words "and 45A(1)(a)". |
| | In section 30B(3), the word "80,". |
| | Section 45A. |
| | In section 56(1), the words "(and in particular to those of section 81 below)". |
| | Section 60(6). |
| | In sections 61(1) and (2), the words "on account of a child or an adult". |
| | In section 63(c) and (f)(i), the words "and child". |
| | In section 77(1), the words following paragraph (b). |
| | In section 78(4)(d), the word "80,". |
| | Sections 80 and 81. |
| | In section 89(1), the words "section 80 and" and, in the heading, the words "child or". |
| | In section 90, the words "child or". |
| | In section 91(1)(b), the words "for an adult dependant". |
| | In section 122(1), in the definition of "week", the words ", except in relation to disabled person's tax credit,". |
| | Section 123(1)(b) and (c). |
| | Sections 128 and 129. |
| | In section 135(5), the words "In relation to income support, housing benefit and council tax benefit,". |
| | Section 145(5). |
| | In section 175(1A), in paragraph (a), the words "of Part 1 or 6 of this Act" and paragraph (b) and the word "and" before it. |
| | In Schedule 4, in Part 4, in column (1), the entries relating to widowed mother's allowance, widowed parent's allowance and child's special allowance and column (2). |
| | In Schedule 5, in paragraph 2(5)(b), the word "80,". |
| | In Schedule 9, paragraph 4. |

| Title and reference | Extent of repeal or revocation |
|---|---|
| Social Security Administration Act 1992 (c. 5) | In section 3(3), the words "(together with any increase under section 80(5) of the Contributions and Benefits Act)". |
| | Section 5(2)(c) and (d). |
| | Section 11. |
| | Section 71(11)(c) and (d). |
| | In section 121DA(1), the words "working families' tax credit, disabled person's tax credit,". |
| | In section 124(2)(b), the words "and working families tax credit". |
| | In section 150, in subsection (1), paragraph (f) and, in paragraph (h), the words "prescribed for the purposes of section 128(5) or 129(8) of that Act or" and subsection (10)(b)(i) and (ii). |
| | Section 154(2)(b) and (c). |
| | Section 163(2)(d)(ii) and (iii). |
| | Section 179(5)(b) and (c). |
| | In section 189(1), the word "other". |
| | In section 191, in the definition of "income-related benefit", paragraphs (b) and (c). |
| Social Security Contributions and Benefits (Northern Ireland) Act 1992 (c. 7) | In section 20(1), the words "(with increase for child dependants)" (in each place) and, in paragraph (f)(i), the words "and child". |
| | In section 21(5A)(b), the words "and 45A(1)(a)". |
| | In section 30B(3), the word "80,". |
| | Section 45A. |
| | In section 56(1), the words "(and in particular to those of section 81 below)". |
| | Section 60(6). |
| | In section 61(1) and (2), the words "on account of a child or an adult". |
| | In section 63(c) and (f)(i), the words "and child". |
| | In section 77(1), the words following paragraph (b). |
| | In section 78(4)(d), the word "80,". |
| | Sections 80 and 81. |

| *Title and reference* | *Extent of repeal or revocation* |
|---|---|
| | In section 89(1), the words "section 80 and" and, in the heading, the words "child or". |
| | In section 90, the words "child or". |
| | In section 91(1)(b), the words "for an adult dependant". |
| | In section 121(1), in the definition of "week", the words ", except in relation to disabled person's tax credit,". |
| | Section 122(1)(b) and (c). |
| | Sections 127 and 128. |
| | In section 131(5), the words "In relation to income support and housing benefit,". |
| | Section 141(5). |
| | In section 172, in subsection (2)(a), the words "or 141" and, in subsection (3)(c), the words "(other than section 141)". |
| | In Schedule 4, in Part 4, in column (1), the entries relating to widowed mother's allowance, widowed parent's allowance and child's special allowance and column (2). |
| | In Schedule 5, in paragraph 2(5)(b), the word "80,". |
| | In Schedule 9, paragraph 4. |
| Social Security Administration (Northern Ireland) Act 1992 (c. 8) | In section 3(3), the words "(together with any increase under section 80(5) of the Contributions and Benefits Act)". |
| | Section 5(2)(c) and (d). |
| | Section 9. |
| | Section 69(11)(c) and (d). |
| | In section 115CA(1), the words "working families' tax credit, disabled person's tax credit,". |
| | Section 134(2)(b) and (c). |
| | Section 155(5)(b) and (c). |
| | In section 167(1), in the definition of "income-related benefit", paragraphs (b) and (c). |
| Local Government Finance Act 1992 (c. 14) | In Schedule 9, paragraphs 2 and 8. |
| Finance Act 1994 (c. 9) | In section 139(1), paragraph (b) and the word "and" before it. |

| *Title and reference* | *Extent of repeal or revocation* |
|---|---|
| Social Security (Incapacity for Work) Act 1994 (c. 18) | Section 2(4). |
| | Section 10. |
| | In Schedule 1, paragraph 32. |
| Social Security (Incapacity for Work) (Northern Ireland) Order 1994 (S.I. 1994/1898 (N.I. 12)) | Article 4(3). |
| | Article 12. |
| | In Schedule 1, paragraph 32. |
| Jobseekers Act 1995 (c. 18) | Section 29(7)(a) and (b). |
| | In Schedule 2, paragraphs 9, 33 and 34. |
| Pensions Act 1995 (c. 26) | Section 127. |
| Children (Scotland) Act 1995 (c. 36) | In section 22(4)(a), the words "or working families' tax credit". |
| Children (Northern Ireland) Order 1995 (S.I. 1995/755 (N.I. 2)) | In Article 2(2), the definitions of "disabled person's tax credit" and "working families' tax credit". |
| | In Article 18C(7)(b), the words ", working families' tax credit or disabled person's tax credit". |
| Jobseekers (Northern Ireland) Order 1995 (S.I. 1995/2705 (N.I. 15)) | Article 31(7)(a) and (b). |
| | In Schedule 2, paragraphs 2, 16 and 17. |
| Pensions (Northern Ireland) Order 1995 (S.I. 1995/3213 (N.I. 22)) | Article 124. |
| Employment Tribunals Act 1996 (c. 17) | Section 21(1)(fg). |
| Employment Rights Act 1996 (c. 18) | Section 192(2)(ab). |
| Employment Rights (Northern Ireland) Order 1996 (S.I. 1996/1919 (N.I. 16)) | Article 237(2)(ab). |
| Finance Act 1997 (c. 16) | Section 110(5AA). |
| Social Security Act 1998 (c. 14) | Section 8(3)(d) and (e). |
| Tax Credits (Initial Expenditure) Act 1998 (c. 16) | The whole Act. |
| Social Security (Northern Ireland) Order 1998 (S.I. 1998/1506 (N.I. 10)) | Article 9(3)(d) and (e). |
| Tax Credits Act 1999 (c. 10) | The whole Act. |
| Finance Act 1999 (c. 16) | Section 30. |
| | Section 31(9) and (12). |
| | Schedule 3. |
| Access to Justice Act 1999 (c. 22) | Section 33. |
| Employment Relations Act 1999 (c. 26) | Section 18(5). |

| *Title and reference* | *Extent of repeal or revocation* |
|---|---|
| | In Schedule 4, paragraph 31(a). |
| Welfare Reform and Pensions Act 1999 (c. 30) | In Schedule 8, paragraphs 11 and 14. |
| Immigration and Asylum Act 1999 (c. 33) | Section 115(1)(f) and (g). |
| Employment Relations (Northern Ireland) Order 1999 (S.I. 1999/2790 (N.I. 9)) | Article 20(5)(b). |
| | In Schedule 4, paragraph 13(a). |
| Welfare Reform and Pensions (Northern Ireland) Order 1999 (S.I. 1999/3147 (N.I. 11)) | In Schedule 8, paragraphs 10 and 13. |
| Finance Act 2000 (c. 17) | Section 34. |
| | In section 84(2), the words "an employment credit or". |
| Government Resources and Accounts Act 2000 (c. 20) | In Schedule 1, paragraph 25. |
| Finance Act 2001 (c. 9) | Sections 52 and 53. |
| | Schedule 11. |
| Social Security Fraud Act 2001 (c. 11) | In section 7(8), in the definition of "disqualifying benefit", paragraph (b)(ii) and (iii). |
| Social Security Fraud Act (Northern Ireland) 2001 (c. 17 (N.I.)) | In section 6(8), in the definition of "disqualifying benefit", paragraph (b)(ii) and (iii). |
| Employment Act 2002 (c. 22) | In Schedules 3, 4 and 5, the entries relating to Schedule 3 to the Tax Credits Act 1999. |
| | In Schedule 6, paragraphs 9 and 10. |
| | In Schedule 7, paragraph 52. |
| Criminal Injuries Compensation (Northern Ireland) Order 2002 (S.I. 2002/796 (N.I. 1)) | Article 12(3). |

Adapted and published by GRANGIS under the OGL Licence 3.0.

www.nationalarchives.gov.uk/doc/open-government-licence/version/3/

GRANGIS - UK PUBLISHING 2022.

Thank you for taking the time to leave us a review regarding this version

★★★★★

For further inquiries, contact us at:
www.grangis.com / contact@grangis.com

www.ingramcontent.com/pod-product-compliance
Lightning Source LLC
LaVergne TN
LVHW060213210926
848481LV00008B/2731